in his Foreword to
Childhood:

Many readers of Jan Myrdal consider him a very Swedish writer, a man like Strindberg tortured by life and the complexity of his own being. This view is correct. Jan Myrdal has deeply confronted the dark urgings of his soul and the role of humanity in a possibly infinite universe.

But, as Myrdal reveals in *Childhood,* he is a boy as well as a man, a child of his times and his society and particularly of his family. Like any serious person, he has devoted much time trying to understand his early years and how he grew into adulthood.

It is his seriousness of purpose and resolute determination which give Myrdal's works their honesty and a truth which can be embarrassing and unexpectedly frank.

Few have tried so hard as Myrdal to understand themselves. At the center of this study lie his parents and his relationship with these Nobel prize winners, Gunnar and Alva Myrdal. It was, as the boy Jan saw it, a brutal relationship and in retrospect he convinces us that the boy was right. Not many children have survived a mother who saw her son as a kind of laboratory animal for behavioral studies and a father who did not conceal his contempt for the being he and his wife had brought into life.

But if Myrdal gives us excruciating scenes with an icy verisimilitude, he also gives us scenes of extraordinary warmth and love—the growing up of a boy who found in his grandparents surrogates suffused with humanity and common sense. With them Myrdal passed ideal days. This, no doubt, is why survived.

Childhood can be read at many levels. To those who have known of Jan Myrdal's painfully impossible relations with his famous parents it provides a coda. When I first read his *Confessions of a Disloyal European,* I thought Jan had exaggerated, there seemed something polymorphous perverse about a middle-aged man coddling such violent reactions. After reading *Childhood* Myrdal's conduct seems natural. There is a harsh reality about *Childhood* that leaves little room for doubt of the trauma. And *Childhood* makes clear Myrdal's view of Sweden's separateness (and his own) from the Europe of Common Markets and common culture. Sweden is apart and away.

Myrdal's *Childhood* is no tale of boggy introspection. It is exciting and even funny, no chapter perhaps more tingling than his adventure on the winter icefloe, leaping from floe to floe, across the Karlberg Canal. Jan and his friends played this dangerous game many times. One morning he went out early. No one was around. The moon was still shining over Karlberg Palace. He missed a jump and went under the ice. To this day he has no recollection of how (or whether) he got out of the water. To this day he wonders whether he really did get out and how can he prove to himself that he is still alive.

This is the kind of question that might have entered Tom Sawyer's mind. It preoccupied the mind of the young Stockholm schoolboy and it still lingers there on cold dark nights of the long Swedish winter.

All his life Jan Myrdal has prided himself on being a maverick. Now this maverick has taken his place in the forefront of Swedish letters.

What U.S. critics said about Jan Myrdal's *Childhood*

"...oddly enough, if the atmosphere of "Childhood" sometimes evokes an Ingmar Bergman film, passions congealing into icy solitude, the overall mood is tender and lyrical. The account traces formation of a self from early consciousness to puberty and is not an autobiography in the ordinary sense, but an unsentimental story about childhood.... The viewpoint of the child with its contrasts of vast space and the intimate detail of familiar rooms, its casual schoolyard cruelties and chance epiphanies (a Zeppelin glittering over the Alps, telephone wires singing), its web of prohibitions and fantasy systems, is acutely rendered. A chapter that begins, "One late winter day I drowned," blends hair-raising reality with the visionary....
—Robert Taylor, Boston Globe

"The son of Swedish Nobel laureates Alva and Gunnar Myrdal, the author *(Confessions of a Disloyal European)* here offers an unsentimental, deeply personal memoir of his childhood from five to eleven. He strips away the social and intellectual pretenses of his famous, worldly parents, revealing their contempt for the "problem child" they believed they had been saddled with. Through exercising brutal candor, Myrdal relates much that is good—magical times spent with his beloved grandparents on their family farm; school friends; mischief-making—as well as the anger and hurt caused by parents who could not seem to love him....Ably translated from the Swedish, this book is straightforwardly and beautifully written, successfully evoking emotions without manipulating the reader.

—Publishers Weekly

"A scandalous best-seller in Sweden in 1982, this bitter portrait of Nobel laureates Gunnar and Alva Myrdal horrified Swedes, who revere the couple as founders of their nation's social democratic system.

"In this country, the book can be appreciated as a painfully accurate rendition of the world view of a lonely, sensitive boy—the way the author insists he intended it to be read.

"Given the current spate of whiny books whose authors seem to enjoy being cringing victims totally unable to help themselvs, it's a pleasure to be reminded that even very young people can be courageous, resourceful individuals capable of asserting their will in a strife-ridden family.

"The horror of child abuse is trivialized by those who place every parental misdeed on a par with incest or regular beatings.

"Jan Myrdal's savagely honest account of his youth escapes the trap of self-pity by showing a boy damaged by his parents' insensitivity, yet strong enough to overcome his hurt by creating his own values and living by them."

—Chicago Sun-Times

"*Childhood* is a bleak tale. It is about the pitiless corrosion of a child's soul but it is also about enduring love and loyalty. First published in Sweden in 1982 to public outcry, it has since become a classic. In this autobiographical novel, Jan Myrdal...tells the story of a childhood in a family torn apart by culture, politics and ambition....a beautifully told tale of the formation of an *I*.

Mr. Myrdal writes in a prose as crystalline as ice and as surreal as melting glass. In heartbreaking scenes, one believs one is watching a small child fight to keep sanity itself under the pressure of overwhelming emotional suffering....For all the tragic outcomes of his personal life and public stances, he has done the impossible. In "Childhood," he has taken an act of private catharsis and public accusation and made of it a gift to world literature. We should be grateful."

—Jessica Gress-Wright, Hoover Institution
Washington Times

About Jan Myrdal

Jan Myrdal's first autobiographical novel, *Childhood,* was a major scandal for its intimate and unsentimental look at the private life of Sweden's intellectual and political establishment. The son of Nobel Laureates Gunnar and Alva Myrdal, founders of the Swedish welfare state and pioneers of progressive social policy, Myrdal was to become not only Sweden's leading writer, but also one of the leading critics of the regime his parents helped create.

Another World, which follows *Childhood* into Myrdal's tenth year, was awarded the Grand Prize for the Novel by Sweden's Literature Foundation; and his third autobiographical novel about childhood, *Twelve Going on Thirteen,* won the Esselte Prize for Literature, with 100,000 copies distributed free to Sweden's middle school seniors. More recently, Myrdal was named by the French government Chevalier des arts et des lettres.

Jan Myrdal is the author of over sixty books—novels, poetry, plays, political and social commentary, history, art and literary criticism, and scholarly editions of Balzac, Diderot and Strindberg. He has also curated art exhibitions, made feature films and numerous television documentaries, and he maintains a constant presence in Swedish life through his often controversial newspaper columns and appearances on radio and television.

Very little of this writing has been translated into English. Readers in the United States know him mainly for *Report from a Chinese Village* ("a social classic"—Harrison Salisbury) and *Confessions of a Disloyal European* (one of ten books of "particular significance and excellence in 1968"—NY Times Book Review).

ESSELTE PRIZE FOR LITERATURE (SWEDEN)

12 GOING ON 13

An autobiographical novel by

JAN MYRDAL

Translated by Christine Swanson

Uncorrected galleys
$19.95 cloth   ISBN 1-884468-01-2

Distributed by Lake View Press.
For more information, contact::
Paul Elitzik
Lake View Press
312/935-2694

RAVENSWOOD BOOKS • CHICAGO

Originally published in Sweden as Tolv på det trettonde
by P.A. Norstedt & Söners Förlag, Stockholm 1989.
Published in 1995.
Printed in the United States of America.

ISBN 1-884468-01-2

C H A P T E R 1

I was twelve then, going on thirteen and soon—in only a few weeks—would be thirteen on the fourteenth. Early in the morning I stood at the railing and waited to see Manhattan's faraway skyline come out of the fog into view. It was 1940. The sun would come up behind me and everything had come to an end. Everything.

The dawn was like thin, gray cotton around the ship. The deck heaved slowly under me. The waves rolled in from the huge Atlantic out there. But there was no freshness in the air. Through the fog came a smell of earth and sewer and old sour salty steam. And here where we were anchored the water far down below wasn't a green churning sea. It was a thick, foul tepid mass of water I saw far below me at the side of the ship. Oil floating on this gray surface rocked listlessly, spread, merged together. I made my right hand into a tube, closed the bad left eye, held the tube in front of the right eye and looked down at the water. The floating oil looked almost like a protoplasmic membrane. Like protozoa through a microscope in science class when we talked about how life had once been able to form in the tepid water along the ocean shore.

And Mr. Laurence would stand in front of us with his feet wide apart and show with words the origin of all history so that it all played out here and now in front of me in the classroom. How the globe swelled and the clouds clung together and the sea rose, but volcanoes still spewed lava and the sun was dimmed by their smoke. There in heat and soot the primeval slime itself was born in photosynthesis when the clouds suddenly scattered and the hard light pushed through. The oil down there was organic too, after all. Old dead primeval animals and ferns rotted in primeval times.

I saw the muted colors play on the dark water as it grew lighter. Out of the hazy dawn four huge smoke-stacks belched on the nearest shore. In the dimness under the cloud of smoke there was a coal power plant. It had a cargo dock for coal barges with three big cranes with gigantic scoops; a track with a small diesel switcher pulling the hopper cars. All around there were a lot of interesting details and if things hadn't been the way they were I would have taken pictures when the fog lifted and used them to draw construction plans. But it wasn't like that any more. Nothing was. The whole thing was over.

But above the power plant the wretchedness on the beach began again. It was littered with rotten poles com-ing up from the gray earth at ebb tide. Abandoned sheds, rusty tracks and heaps of trash. There were rats, even if I wasn't near enough to see them. And beside all of it was the gigantic power plant spewing smoke. None of this could be seen through the still boiling gray haze. But it didn't matter that water and morning fog still rolled together gray in gray and offended the eyes and that naked smokestacks appeared belching above. I knew how it was. I had seen it.

The whole day before, starting when they began to load barrels from the dock out here yesterday morning, I had kept myself locked up in my cabin and this miserable shoreline was my only view. From my cabin I could glimpse the power plant. When I pulled the red and white curtains aside and looked through the porthole I saw this dirty waterfront. I kept myself locked up all day and didn't even go to meals. The steward had brought me six bottles of Coca-Cola and a package of Ritz saltines they didn't know about. When they knocked and pulled at the door I said I was reading. And I was too. I was reading Mark Twain and was a Yankee who in spite of technical knowhow and modern science was defeated by the wretched knights of old ignorant churchgoing Europe. Or a Jim who pretended to be a royal prisoner, although he could maybe open the door when he wanted. And when I wasn't reading I lay in the berth and juggled with an empty Coca-Cola bottle and fantasized. I was somewhere other than here. And it didn't do them any good to put on airs and chirp and it didn't help to tug and pull at the door and get angry. True, they had brought me here, but then I had closed myself in and I could lock the steel door and I had fixed it so they had to stand there.

If I let go of the railing, turned and lifted my eyes I should be able to see the sun rise, I thought. But I couldn't do that. It was hidden in the morning fog over the ocean, and looked like a red streak in the bank of clouds. But the water was changing colors and

Manhattan appeared.

Sure, I could have opened the door yesterday—it was called a door even though the window was called a porthole. But I hadn't done it. As soon as I was brought on board I had seen I could lock myself in. I did that yesterday. I had gone up on deck while they were still sleeping. When the fog lifted the windows glittered over there in New York. A new day was beginning over there; an ordinary Wednesday when Nelson and the others ate breakfast and were going to school. But what good did it do to think about that? Even if I took a big jump and dove in from the deck to swim back home to Manhattan I wouldn't make it. I wouldn't be able to do it.

Yes, I was good at diving and swimming. It was the only thing like that I could do well. I just didn't participate in basketball and baseball and other things. No one had been able to make me, either. But I could dive. Like a seal, Uncle Folke had said two summers before. And I could swim a long way down under the water. But if I dove from the deck down into the foul water I would never make it. I would be sucked down into the oil, cough from the foul-smelling sewage which would make me sick when I couldn't help taking a gulp. I would get cramps and drown like a kitten long before I reached land. My hair would get matted with tar and green with slimy algae. They would have to send out the police boats or maybe even a harbor tug to search for me as I floated away with the tide, my mouth gaping and eyes wide open.

And even if I did reach land it would only be the

*Passages written in English in the Swedish edition are in italics.

shore under the power plant. They would have radioed from the command center when I got up out of the water and tried to get hold of the slippery rotting boards that were once a cargo pier. Then I would would lift my eyes and look! the whole shoreline was blue with police. Police and dogs. I threw myself backward into the water and tried to escape by ducking and swimming in under the old dock and bullets came hissing into the water around me. Choff! Choff! I went deeper to escape but was forced up toward the surface to breathe and a big Irish cop who was just waiting there smiled faintly as he shot. Then I lay and floated in the foul water with head crushed and blood mixed with oil and they pulled the body up with a boat-hook.

*"He got what he deserved!"** *

Whatever I did they would bring me in. There is no hiding place.

It was early Wednesday morning, May 7, 1940, and I was on board the MS *Mathilda Thordén*. It would be the second day the boat was anchored in the upper bay outside New York. It was a Finnish line and we would carry war materiel to Finland. There had been peace there for several months but war would probably come soon and what Finland didn't need Sweden would get. Planes were packed in large wooden crates and they had been loaded at the pier before we got on board.

Our car had also been put on board together with the planes. It was a big eight-cylinder Hudson. Gunnar had bought it cheap the year before. He had only paid about what two ordinary Chevrolets cost, even though it was worth as much as the next-to-the-biggest Packard. He bargained the price down to $1100 when it was the luxury model of 1937 because the new automatic transmission on that model had some bugs in it. They had altered the design already by 1938. But it was roomy, with space for eight people if they squeezed together. That car was for Per Albin, our prime minister, Gunnar said. It could be used as an official government car or military staff car in the war. There was a fold-out table and everything in the back seat. There they could spread out their maps when the war started in Sweden.

But now the MS *Mathilda Thordén* couldn't stay at the pier any longer because we were loading barrels with explosives for the Finns' new war. There were special firemen on the dock when the barrels came. As the barrels came on board I told Sissela we certainly wouldn't need to do the life boat drill on this trip.

"It wouldn't even take a torpedo or a floating mine. A U-boat captain would only need to shoot a small hole in the barrels there on the deck. A single hit with a bullet in one of those barrels and it would be all over. Choff! Bang! Vroom! You would be blown to bits and die before you could hiccough and there wouldn't be so much as a fingernail left of you." That's the kind of boat it was.

"Jan!" said Alva. "Don't say things like that. You're scaring her."

"But it's the truth," I said. "You put us on a boat like this for the sake of honor, your public image and reputation. You know it, but you don't dare say so."

The cargo was all war materiel and therefore contraband, so we couldn't get safe-conduct.

"It'll look great if it happens at night," I said. "A huge red fountain out in the middle of the Atlantic. Like a volcanic eruption. And there won't be so much as the nail of a little finger left of the children to bury.

"And no one to come with flowers and wreaths and make speeches and bury them either because everything would be blown to kingdom come," I added.

Then I left them standing on the deck and hurried away from there before Alva could think of an answer.

Only a week before I had gone to school as usual. We weren't going to Sweden any more. It had been decided. We would stay in America. They for the duration and I forever. The family would move away from Riverside Drive in the fall. They had sublet the apartment furnished.

First they had looked at apartments on Central Park. The parents of some of my classmates had large apartments there. Like the Rosenthals. I had hardly ever seen old man Rosenthal when I visited because he was there only occasionally. Most of the time he was in Washington with Roosevelt. But then Gunnar rented a real house in Brooklyn with a little yard and everything. I had been there to see it when they decided. I would have a room with sun in the afternoon and two walls of bookshelves and space for a big desk and also a special room for the model railroad up in the attic. I hadn't been able to start building it there on Riverside Drive, where we wouldn't be staying more than about a year and there was no room where I could put nails in the walls. If we had moved to Central Park it would have been too expensive to let me have a room for the railroad. This spring it was called "The Rusty Springs Railroad Corporation." But since last summer, when it didn't have a real name yet, I had been designing various possible layouts and building cars and different structures and I already had two locomotives too. A 4-6-4 Hudson I had bought in the spring of 1939 and an 0-4-0 switcher from Mantua which I got this January. The Hudson was actually an American Flyer and almost tin-plate, but I had put the switcher together myself and painted it.

Ever since it had been decided that we would move to Brooklyn and the railroad would have its own place up there in the attic, I had worked on the track layout for this room with a sloping ceiling and chimney. Layouts where the train went around in circles or figure eights were childish even if they were called models and supposedly built to scale. Toy railroads around the Christmas tree on Christmas Eve! About like Irving, the Burns boy, with his Lionel train which he was allowed to take out only on holidays and put on the floor with his father sitting beside him. Because:

"We are such great pals!"

And it was Mr. Burns himself who operated the rheostat and Irving only got to place the cars back on the track when the speed was too much for the curves and the train derailed.

The sloping ceiling, the chimney and steps up were a given. I would make use of them in the plans. The sloping ceiling gave extra track possibilities if I made a city street for a background with buildings going all the way up to the ceiling for example. Several side-tracks could be hidden behind them. This was worth thinking about. It would be ridiculous to pretend to have a big transcontinental railroad in an attic. Then the whole thing became only a toy even if the one who built it was an old man of fifty and went around with an engineer's cap on his head. You could make it a piece of reality instead and create a view at the front of the room which almost looked real and have the track disappear from the scene through tunnels under the streets or something and make it look real and the whole big network of tracks like something to read about in timetables and believe in. That's how it was in the real world too. You saw only a piece of it at a time and heard about the rest. Who could see all of New York at one time?

But "Rusty Springs Railroad Corporation" was not a big line like the New York Central. It wasn't even a medium-sized railroad like the Chicago and Northwestern. My RSRRC was a railroad that ran irregularly. Its heyday was in the 1910s. And I would build its railroad yard and the various industrial tracks from the outskirts of the city to the harbor. Rusty Springs was a very small town somewhere out west on the Great Lakes.

In school I had been working on a project about the steam revolution and the big railroad era since the beginning of fall semester and we had come back to New York after summer vacation. It was even more fun than the volcanoes we had studied the year before. It was a current topic too. I didn't agree with General Motors, even though their Futurama was excellent, and thought the age of the railroad was not over at all. Railroads made more sense than cars. There was after all less friction with rails than with highways.

Now it was already tomorrow and nature always chooses the shortest way and technology is forced to take the long way—no matter what the individual believes or wants—to the most energy efficient solution, I thought Mr. Flourens said when I discussed the project with him. Development drives us all inevitably forward, but he who studies nature and learns its laws will reach the goal sooner than he who is forced to follow its requirements, resisting and struggling—*kicking like a small child.*

I saw him in front of me. Mr. Flourens was old, more than fifty, maybe over sixty, and bald with a pot-belly and gold chain draped diagonally across his vest like the one Grandfather had. He didn't talk like other teachers. Not only because he spoke English with a funny accent. Several of the teachers were immigrants who spoke with strange accents. Many of them had fled Europe and European universities when Hitler came to power. But Mr. Flourens wasn't a refugee, he was an immigrant. But I don't know whether he bothered to become a citizen even though he had been here since before the Great War, as he called it. He was actually from France. What was different about his speech was that he talked the way they write in books. He used much bigger words than other people. And he was different from all the other teachers also because he didn't care if someone said he didn't understand.

"Go then, my young friend, to the library, take a dictionary and look it up. Baby birds sit in the nest with open beaks and cry. You are still a child, but will soon be a man! No one can give you the word, the knowledge, you don't conquer yourself. But then you have the knowledge. While others run around trying to learn through trial and error you can, with its help, think and in one well-considered action seek the answer with the least possible expenditure of energy. But remember that the knowledge you get from teachers and books is old knowledge. It can already be moldy. Therefore you should, like a smart boy, learn both what I as your teacher tell you and what you read in books and then doubt it and see if it isn't already wrong.

"*De omnibus dubitandum!*" he said and tapped my head with his knuckles. "Keep that in mind."

But he may have said:

"*Doubt everything at least once.* Even the assertion that two plus two equals four."

Then he would be laughing already and talking about dyadic arithmetic.

None of the other teachers said things like that. No one behaved as he did. They explained simple words and were nice. And even if they weren't Christians, you couldn't really ask: But on the other hand? Because: *He that doubteth is damned.* But, I thought, Mr. Flourens told us when he introduced himself that he wasn't a teacher, but a bridge builder with big firms that did steel construction in Chicago as well as New York. He had long been interested in how design sense could be awakened and analytical intelligence could be ignited in children. In his later years, with his family finances in order and his children grown and leading their own lives, he went to Teachers College at Columbia University. Now he planned to try his theories on us.

Last fall when I first met him in the library, and later when I was in his class he talked a lot about friction and energy and even demonstrated that the idea of a perpetual motion machine contradicted the laws of reason.

When I sat in the library and talked with him about my railroad history he had said that if I intended to write something I shouldn't focus just on the small details of the events, but also on the internal relationships.

"Take the history of the rail, for example. The track width is historically determined, but still accidental. It is the Roman distance between wheels. The one they used in their roadways. And so that accident became a historical necessity. A few inches more or less wouldn't have made any difference at the beginning. The step from road to railroad wasn't difficult. Rain and mud became ooze into which the wheel sank. When the railroad was invented it kept the same dimensions. The basic principle was that the rails' smoothness and limited surface area in comparison with the unavoidably irregular roadway offered less friction and therefore saved energy. That rails were cost-effective had been proven in the coal fields of Newcastle since the end of the eighteenth century. On rails of wood a horse could pull a load down to the river weighing four times what was possible on a road. But wood wore down quickly. Throughout the nineteenth century these wooden rails were developed into iron railways without difficulty, step by step. Rails were invented this way out of simple necessity. But what happened in the steam age when a leap was made and the horse-drawn carts on these new rails of iron were replaced with self-propelled steam engines? Even the great engineers were caught up in the prejudices of their limited experience like chickens by a chalk line! Think carefully about that!

"Go West young man and grow up with the country!
"Go, young man, to the library and read!

I did that because we had a good library at Lincoln School. But it took several days before I was sure I had really understood it all. When I read carefully I realized that you could take as an instructive example—one to which Mr. Flourens sometimes referred—the rail designs for Trevithick and Vivian's steam locomotive for the mining operation at Merthyr-Tydvil in 1804 and what they wrote about the role of friction. Trevithick and Vivian were good engineers. They had developed the steam-driven road-traveling cars, long in experimental use in France and America, into a genuine steam carriage which they patented in 1801. But when they tried to put a steam-powered car on the rails and replace horses as the power source in the mine railroad, they made an effort to make the rail's friction the same as that of the road. They were convinced—as they wrote—that between two plane surfaces the adhesion is too weak. The vehicle is subject to gliding, the wheels spin and the propelling force is lost. But this was all wrong. Their thinking went astray there! They were unable to see that the rolling wheel's friction is a strong counter-force, adhesion, and not the weak gliding friction. Their thinking didn't follow along in the leap from the horse-drawn car to the self-propelling one.

"Their failure in reasoning can also easily be committed by a little child like you," Mr. Flourens said to me across the library table when I looked up from the books and told him what I had found.

And the lesson in this, he said, was that the obvious error which I as a twelve-year-old had easily uncovered was totally invisible to the great and famous scientists of those days.

"This aberration of established scientific opinion shows very well what results theoretical convictions can have if they are simply accepted as truth and do not rest on the basis of experimental reason. A whole generation of engineers tried, like Trevithick, to overcome difficulties which existed only in the imaginary world of science. The problem wasn't solved until 1813 when Blackett of Wigan Railroad asked the question which should have been asked in the beginning and sought the answer as it should be sought, with an experiment. He found the locomotive's own weight created the necessary friction.

"But," said Mr. Flourens, "don't laugh at their stupidity! Blenkinsop's energy-greedy rack rail locomotive and

Brunton's locomotive propelled with levers like horses' feet were attempts by serious engineers to overcome difficulties. It was just that the difficulties to be overcome existed only in their imaginations. They followed common-sense reasoning. They thought in terms of horse-age truths about vehicles which were passively pulled along. But the steam age had arrived. Now the rules were changed. The future belonged to a new truth. The truth of the self-propelled vehicle. What already obsolete truths are you and I thinking a hundred years later, in 1940, in this library at Lincoln School, Teacher's College, Columbia University, New York City? What in our work will our successors find unbelievably nonsensical?

"Do you think you are smarter than Trevithick? You are only living 136 years later! The young always know more than the old," he said. "But they are, on the other hand, seldom as wise!" he added and indicated with a gesture that I should laugh.

Henry Ford, who understood mass production, didn't understand the secret of the rails either, I thought later. And one of Hitler's big mistakes was replacing railways with highways. Kalmbach wrote about that in his article in *The Model Railroader* when the war began, and he was right.

The steam engine was not the most effective, I knew that. Its efficiency was low. It could utilize a maximum of just 18 percent of the heat. Even the best locomotive operated far under the limit. We were already living far into the age of the electrical revolution and soon we would free the powerful energy of the atom, as

Mr. Flourens said while I sat in the library and read about the atom-smasher at Westinghouse Laboratories in East Pittsburgh, Pennsylvania. But the steam locomotive was beautiful, I thought, and besides, I would be the one to decide the time and place of the model world I wanted. I was not going to have the city come up out of the Depression and make the train more economical. Because of that, I didn't need to electrify the RSRRC or build a diesel locomotive. While I was still working on the whole age of the railroad, to make sure I didn't go wrong when I started to build, I wrote out the history of Rusty Springs as it might have been done in one of those Federal Writers' Projects on its centennial in 1937. I had hunted up pictures which would probably have fit and everything. The story did not really belong to the project, it was just pretend. But I wrote so you couldn't tell what was genuine railroad history and what I had thought up. The seams shouldn't show. She, Miss Evans in Social Science, who really existed, wondered where Rusty Springs was when she read what I wrote and praised it. She had believed it!

I had thought up the city when I got home from Minnesota. I worked on it on the train down to Chicago. I was already partway into the project on the age of the railroad, and knew where I could fit it in. I named my model railway the RSRRC then. Before that, in the fall of 1939, I thought the railroad I would build would be most like the commuter line on Long Island and I spent the whole summer documenting it in photographs and on film. I had used the time out on Long Island to make sure I got a complete photographic record of the Long Island Railroad's rolling stock, its signal system and its rail yard. I had started by going along with Karna in June 1939 when she drove to Greenlawn to shop. The family spent summer vacation fifty miles out on Long Island in a large house with a fantastic view of the ocean. It was completely protected from sight by a real vineyard and its own swimming beach. It was called Ercildoune and was located outside Centerport and there were millionaires living all around, Vanderbilts and all the others, and Greenlawn was the closest station. While Karna was shopping I took photographs and home movies.

Later in the summer she drove around with me to various stations on the Long Island Railroad. She thought it was fun to drive now that she had her American driver's license. I sat beside her on the front seat and read the map while she drove. Because of this it was good that Gunnar and Alva were away traveling almost all the time that summer. They were down South and out West and usually didn't even leave their address. Gunnar said Karna was capable and could take care of the house and me and the little girls and everything with Ingrid. If there were problems she could talk to his secretary. Miss Dornbrush was her name and she was helpful. But when Gunnar left the car on Long Island so Karna could shop, we could take it whenever we wanted and drive all over to the places where I needed to document the railroad without having to ask permission. Karna had the window beside her rolled down when she drove. The wind ruffled her hair. She wasn't wearing her hair at the back of her neck now, only a ribbon to keep the hair out of her eyes.

"Is this where we turn off?" she asked.

"No," I said. "Not until the next intersection in two miles." I had the map and knew where we should go. Her arms were suntanned and she was wearing her new blue and white summer dress with a small flower print and white collar. It wasn't really a dress, but a kind of cleaning smock with big buttons all the way down the front.

"Now you decide," she said.

Down at the Five-and-Ten Cent Store diagonally across from the Nemo movie theater a few blocks down Broadway I had found scrapbooks when we were in town before packing for summer vacation. They weren't especially nice. They were shiny and embossed with flowers in relief. *SCRAP BOOK* it said diagonally across the cover in ornate letters. But they were cheap and I bought two green and two black ones. I gave one of the black ones the title: *Prototype Material.* I wrote that with a broad pen on the first page and drew a blue frame around it. Then I began to paste. First I pasted in a general track diagram for the whole Long Island Railroad network that I had cut out of a timetable. After that I took the stations and factories section by section. Finally I drew track plans for each station Karna and I visited. When we came home from the railroad excursions I went into the little darkroom I had set up under the stairway and developed the pictures. Then I drew track plans for each station or factory and pasted in the photographs where they should be.

But when I had been up in the Twin Cities and was on the way to Chicago again I was no longer satisfied with Long Island. I had seen bigger factories than the ones Miss Evans used to take us to. Noisier and more chaotic and even bloodier too, like slaughterhouses. I wanted to make something which was more realistic, smokier, with more old bricks and things and made up Rusty Springs because it wasn't possible to build even a model of Chicago.

The newly invented railroad would offer more possibilities than the stations on Long Island. Rusty Springs was an industrial town after all. It lived. The layout would be almost like at the World's Fair, only much, much smaller, of course. So I started a new scrapbook. A blue one. I gave it the title: *Rusty Springs: Ideas and Plans*. I didn't draw any frame this time, though. In this scrapbook I pasted railroad pictures from newspapers and magazines and even the pictures I took in the winter. Some of the track maps were real drawings on graph paper, drawings which could be folded and pasted in. It looked really good.

Now in these large-size drawings I had worked on in the evenings a railroad had evolved with a real locomotive terminal and all its workshops and yards. A terminal for a railroad that served the oil refinery and the slaughterhouse as well as the auto factory. It also had a harbor where the products were shipped out. I had seen a lot of this when our class went on a bus trip around New York and New Jersey with Miss Evans in Social

Science. We learned how the city worked with courts and waterworks and toilets and went on walks in the underworld below Times Square to see what there was under the streets. We went to the auto factory on the other side of the river and the foreman took us around and showed us how cars were put together on the assembly line. We looked at *slum clearance* and visited black families who had been given new apartments and we were taken to see the new schools for slum children. I decided to build some of these facilities I looked at with the school. But not what was under the streets, that was too complicated, and not *slum clearance*. Rusty Springs was not yet in the New Deal, but in decline just as before, and I had also thought about building a real Hooverville of sheds. There ought to be something between the industrial tracks and street facades in the background set up on a shelf so the tunnels would have room to go into the mountainside under the city streets. It should be a really horrible slum with small shacks made of empty boxes and roofs of corrugated sheet-metal, like the ones they didn't take us to see, but I had seen from the bus window when the class was going to the oil refinery in New Jersey.

I had help building the oil refinery and the locomotive yard in the school workshop from plans in Lionel's *The Model Builder* although I recalculated the measurements from "O" gauge to "HO" gauge and altered the whole thing a little to fit in with my railroad. I would build the rest of it all by myself later from the photos and drawings I had made.

By planning the railroad this way I could get a kind of realistic prototype in spite of everything. Times were hard in Rusty Springs and the Depression was hitting the town quite hard, but I could keep the railroad sensibly operational carrying real loads from the harbor and factories. Put together real trains in the railroad yard and then send the trains into a tunnel under the city. Behind there were tracks you couldn't see and I could make timetables and pretend that the train served both mining towns and big cattle towns far inland.

There had been much more to write about Rusty Springs than that it was a grim little town which had once hoped to become a Chicago, but had been passed by in the eighties and fell further behind in the twenties when Detroit grew and then was hit by the Depression. The city had only one newspaper and it was corrupt, as Upton Sinclair showed in *The Brass Check*, and politics were controlled from the smoky back rooms of the Democratic machine which grew extra strong with the help of its bootlegger contacts during Prohibition. The machine resisted Roosevelt's New Deal and I thought about having a group of citizen activists expose the situation to a special federal prosecutor to clean up the city. The crime rate was going up too and that wasn't good for the railroad. I would also trade away the Hudson locomotive as soon as possible. It looked too much like it belonged to the New York Central or some such really big line with a Hudson 4-6-4. RSRRC couldn't afford such a thing, but I wanted a 4-4-2 Atlantic for commuter traffic. They were beautiful.

Now the railroad would never be built. When they told me to pack my bags I just shoved the books in at the last minute. I left the rest. I didn't even really get started on the model of the industrial area I was building at school. They would have to be left unfinished. They were of no use any more. Nothing was of any use any more. Not the RSRRC either. It was all over with that too.

Summer was already over although it was still only May. Nelson and I had sat in my room and made plans for the coming summer until he had to go home the evening I found out.

Nelson and I were going to a camp in Vermont. He had relatives there. Two uncles, one was a Methodist pastor and the other was a realtor who bought and sold houses. His cousin Edgar told us about the camp. I didn't say anything to Alva. She might begin asking too many questions. But if you could talk Gunnar into granting permission, it would stick. Alva wouldn't contradict him. So for me it was just a matter of waiting for the right opportunity to say something about it to Gunnar. He wasn't home much because he traveled a lot and when he was in New York he and Alva usually ate out. Either at a restaurant so they could talk in peace and quiet or they were invited out.

He could get angry too, just sputter if I said it in a way that irritated him. After that it would be extremely difficult to get him to change. If I thought the whole thing through carefully in advance and said the right words, it might work. One Sunday dinner when they were eating at home and he was in a good mood because work was going well and Bunche had written a good paper for him and because of that he kissed Alva's hand in the middle of dinner and called her darling time after time and said we should be happy to have such a good Alva for a mother, I said that Wheelers had offered to take me with Nelson to stay with their relatives at a camp in Vermont this summer.

I knew that Gunnar hadn't intended to rent a summer house on Long Island this year. He and Alva had talked about it several times. It had become both expensive and complicated the year before and they didn't have any Swedes working in the house any more and they weren't planning any big summer parties. They themselves would work in New York and maybe spend some time on the West Coast if it got intolerably hot. They hadn't said anything about me and I don't know what they planned to do with Sissela and Kaj. Maybe I hadn't been listening very closely. Maybe they would place the kids with some of their friends in New England. Now he answered me:

"Yes, it would be good for you to show some initiative and learn to take care of yourself. You're growing up now."

It had been agreed that I would go with Nelson and the others to Vermont, so Nelson and I were planning our summer.

Of course, I hadn't told them everything about the camp. I only told them as much as necessary to get them to go along with the idea. It was a wilderness camp for boys with tenting, fishing, hunting and long hikes in the woods. And a little pre-military training. But I hadn't said anything at all about the military side of camp life and that was mostly for the older boys. The ones who were already out of junior high.

But it was important. There was war in China and war in Europe. Nelson had experienced war himself in China. He had been there during the bombings and had seen real beheadings and how people fell down and died of starvation in the streets and how prisoners were taken away chained together and everything. His parents had worked in Nanking. I had read books like Dos Passos' *Three Soldiers* and Ludwig Renn's *War* in English and Remarque's *All Quiet on the Western Front* in Swedish and had seen lots of newsreels and collected *Life* so I knew what was happening in Europe when the war started this time.

"It was because the Americans didn't have any basic military training that so many died at one time when they came to the front in the previous war," said Nelson now as we discussed the camp. You have to learn how to take cover. My uncle, who is a veteran, always told me so."

I had a small American radio. It was black with chrome trim and streamlined design, but it didn't have short wave. At night when I lay awake I used to listen to different stations. We had so many in New York that you didn't need short wave. I had the volume low and kept the door closed. I couldn't let them hear I was awake. They would have taken away the radio. They didn't know I was often awake for a while in the middle of the night. Especially when I had had a dream. Early in the morning I heard on the radio that the Germans had invaded Denmark and Norway, I awakened Alva and told her what had happened.

"No! No!," she said.

Japan and Germany just marched on. We continued to help Japan by exporting scrap iron and things. We had discussed current events in school. Nelson thought—and he was right—that it was more than a scandal. It endangered our lives. Japan wasn't just conquering China. Japan wanted to conquer the whole world and the Japanese emperor would put his soldiers against us too in the end if we didn't decide to stop him by helping China in a serious way. Almost everyone in the class agreed on that. We were also in agreement that Hitler was not only bad for the Jews and carried out pogroms as the Russian Czar had done before, but also that he was a direct threat to us in America. Not because we would have to get into this war in Europe. None of us really wanted to do that, because most of us believed in spite of everything that it was Europe's war.

I thought Mr. Francis had been right last fall. We had probably been lured into the previous war by the big banking houses. Mr. Francis was gone from school since the war in Finland and we didn't talk about him in the classroom. I remembered him, though, and so did Theobald. We all knew what the British are like, said Theobald. Ireland and India and things like that. Now the British were supporting the Fascists in Mexico against President Cardenas, who was the people's man. Most of the class thought Cardenas was some kind of Communist, like the ham-and-eggs agitators in California, and that the Mexicans had stolen our oil fields. I thought the ham-and-eggs movement in California was about like Per Albin in Sweden and probably good. I was also the only one who agreed with Theobald that the Mexicans had a right to their own oil both according to old Spanish law and Mexican law and ought to defend the rights against the British and our oil companies. I also thought Hitler was seeking world power too, like the Japanese emperor. There were many in the class who didn't agree with that. Now that Hitler had brought on the war in Europe, we ought to help England and France, said Theobald. They were democracies in spite of everything and the rest of the class agreed. It was just Lindbergh and people like him who were isolationist and we didn't have any of those in our class. But just help with credits and export permits and not go to war ourselves, of course.

It was good that there would be pre-military training. We might be drawn into the war eventually after all and I was almost a citizen already. I had my first papers and would soon become a real American and that carried obligations. It was like Uncle Albert said. He was not my uncle, but great-uncle because he was Grandfather's brother, only he had changed his name from Pettersson to Lundkvist when he emigrated 54 years ago. America was a country worth defending. In spite of everything it wasn't like Europe where there was no freedom and they fought all the time. If this war in

Europe lasted as long as the last one and we finally got involved, I would be old enough to be in it. But now everything was over.

I stood at the railing and now that the morning fog had lifted, the gray water came to life and its oily surface broke up and rippled and sparkled away toward Manhattan's skyline and there was no city in the whole world like New York and no country like America!

When Great-Uncle Albert Lundkvist came home from his visit to the Baptist convention in the old country and caught sight of New York coming out of the dimness, he fell on his knees to praise the Lord who had made it possible for him to become an American. A citizen of the United States of America. He had told me that last winter when I told him I was going to be an American too.

Suddenly that evening a week ago after I had walked Nelson to the door and was on my way down the hall to my room, the door to the living room opened behind me and Gunnar came out and called me and asked all of us to come, the small children too. Alva stood beside him on the white carpet between the sofas and he told us he had arranged for him and her and the whole family to go to Sweden in a few days.

"Now start packing," he said.

"Why are we going to Sweden?" I asked.

"I can't tell you that," he said. "You'll find out gradually."

He had probably received some kind of invitation, I assumed. As far as I was concerned they could leave, but

I would stay here. I would stay at my school, they had said that when I was about to get my first papers. That was enough. I didn't need a special room for the model railroad or a railroad or even my own room or anything if only I could stay here at home in America to finish school.

"I can stay," I said. "You don't need to worry about me."

"Don't talk nonsense," said Gunnar. "Now just do as I say."

At first I was going to protest. I already had my mouth open. Then I understood, and I didn't bother to say anything then. That wouldn't be a good idea.

"Don't talk back!" he would answer.

If I said anything right away he and Alva would only get stubborn. It was important to be smart now, to be quiet and make sure they didn't say anything they would have to stick to. It was always like that, but this time it was more important than ever. Now it was a matter of life itself, I thought when Gunnar looked at me, waiting for me to say something more so he could get angry.

But if I showed them I was able to make my own arrangements, they could give in without losing face. I had to be careful and use the right words.

"Now I've solved it," I said the next day.

And I had indeed been able to organize things so I could stay even if they left. It hadn't been at all difficult to arrange. I explained that. I could board with the Lundkvists in Minnesota if we asked them. Or I could go

to boarding school. But I hadn't called Willmar and not
St. Paul either. I hadn't had time for that. And maybe
Alva and Gunnar would think they couldn't afford to let
me stay behind in America. I didn't want to ask them
about that. But now I could tell them there were two
other families who had offered to take charge of me. I
had already asked and they had answered. They had
wealthy friends, the Davenports, with whom they had
spent weekends and who used to talk to me and even
before hearing we were going to Sweden, they had
talked to Alva when she complained about me. They
said I was intelligent and polite and well behaved and
now when I called and asked if they were willing to
help me they said I was a real little American and they
thought it would be a shame to take me out of school
and they certainly could take me in for the duration.

"*In loco parentis!*"

Nelson's parents had also offered to take care of me
if necessary because I wanted so badly to stay here.

"*Of course.* Now that the war is on we have to help
each other."

But it didn't work. They didn't like that I showed I
could arrange to stay. They were upset that I had called
around. I had gone behind their backs. The trip was a
secret.

"You must never tell other people things about us.
You are never to talk to others about the family," said
Alva. "You know that. Never!"

"This foolishness that you should stay here in
America is not to be discussed," said Gunnar.

They said no to everything I had proven I could arrange. What was decided was decided. It couldn't be changed just because of me.

Alva came to my room later. She started to talk about how much I really longed for Sweden and Stockholm and Bromma and all my friends. She knew how it was. I was so homesick that I was ashamed of my own homesickness. That was why I had told Gunnar I wanted to stay in America. I had made him sad. He was worried. I didn't answer her, but continued to read the detective novel I had borrowed from Nelson, *Warrant for X,* by Philip MacDonald. I didn't even look up when she talked to me or show any sign at all that I had noticed her coming into the room. Her voice changed suddenly. She told me I was behaving in a typical pre-adolescent obstinate manner. Then she changed her voice again and said softly that it was nothing to worry about. The main thing was to get me a thyroid medicine to control my weight. But now I was going home to my own friends again and I would get back into my usual group. She understood me, she said. When news comes suddenly people close up like this. It would be better for me if I showed my sadness and let myself cry a little. She understood how I felt. I could pack later when it started to pass. Deep inside I knew I wanted to go home to Sweden. She even tried to hold my head so a chill went through my shoulders and down my back. But not one breath showed I had noticed she was in the room. To come and tell me I really was homesick for Sweden!

I wasn't. I was an American. After a while I got up

from the chair, put the book aside and went through the hall to their room and up to where she sat at the desk. I looked her right in the eye and said I didn't belong to their family any more and I didn't care what they said I wasn't part of it any more. Then I turned, closed the door behind me, walked through the corridor back to my room, closed the door and continued to read. Then I closed my ears to avoid hearing even though she stood there on the floor and talked and gestured with her hands.

"You've got to talk some sense into him," Alva said to Gunnar later in the evening, after I had refused to start packing and stood in front of them one more time and said I was going to stay no matter what they said or did.

"Of course it would be possible to arrange for you to stay and we could probably afford it, but that's not the issue," said Gunnar. "It's a moral question. We come from peasant stock, we don't flee the country in times of danger. It would look bad if we left you here in America in wartime. It would be immoral for us to leave you here. It would imply that we were seeking privileges for ourselves."

He was a Social Democrat and neither accepted aristocratic honors nor sought advantages for his offspring, he said. Alva said I shouldn't forget that many Swedes looked up to the family and saw them as examples.

They had been saying that as long as I could remember and I had maybe believed them when I was little, though the other relatives didn't really. I had become angry and defended them to Aunt Elsa and Aunt Greta when they were sarcastic and said they didn't care what the parents of my friends in Olovslund said about the Myrdals. But it wasn't like that any more, though I was prepared to defend Roosevelt and Per Albin and Cardenas in school.

Now I knew how it really was with all that stuff they talked about. Being examples and having responsibility and behaving like common people. That was for show. What they meant was that no one must know how they were when they weren't on stage.

Yes, I had known that already when we lived in Sweden, but I hadn't wanted to think about it when Aunt Greta talked about them with pursed lips and people laughed about them at the coffee table. That business about examples was just something they said they believed. They said that to each other and to me when they wanted to make me do something. Their friends flattered them by saying it.

"My Little Hypocrite," Gunnar used to say to Sissela, whom he liked. He liked hypocrisy. They were hypocrites. That was the word. Hypocrisy!

I looked at Gunnar and imagined what he might say to Alva when they were alone:

"Darling, today we were examples again."

"Yes, my prince," she would answer. "Today we have been democratic examples for all of Sweden by not falling for the upper class temptation to let Jan stay at his school in New York."

"Oh, darling," Gunnar would say. "The whole people think I am a great genius and you a genuine living angel, so true, so good, so noble."

"Alva is a good person," he used to tell me if he heard me say anything against her. "So good! You've made her sad. You should be ashamed."

Ashamed! But I knew. I knew, so I was ashamed.

None of my classmates here in New York had parents who paid such low wages as Alva and Gunnar paid Karna and Ingrid, whom they took along from Sweden. Most of them had no household help and no babysitter at all. Here it wasn't like it was in Sweden.

Professors and people like that here in America couldn't afford household help. Gunnar earned much more than they did. But if they paid only $25 a month, as Alva paid Ingrid, all of my classmates' parents could have afforded household help even if they earned only American professors' salaries.

I was ashamed when people in the neighborhood talked about how they treated their Swedish help. Even the elevator boys talked about it. But they themselves didn't understand anything:

"We're just good friends," said Alva. "Here no one is master and no one is servant. The girls are here to study and improve themselves and help out a little around the house. We're like a small Swedish colony in a foreign country. We are co-workers, but with different duties in the same household." And she told me that the girls who came along from Sweden to study and who helped out at home too, ate with them and their Swedish guests and they all went to the theater together.

When Alva came into the kitchen last fall all excited and chirping after shopping at Macy's, she twirled around like a model and showed her new clothes to Karna, and Karna said nothing. She pretended she had to see about the children. But afterward, when Alva had gone to her room and we were alone, Karna was white in the face and said:

"She's a professional woman and has secretaries to make her studies easier and I bring coffee to her bedside when it's time for her to wake up and I get $33 a month and work from six in the morning until eight in the evening. And when am I supposed to have time to start my university program? For herself she buys $800 worth of fancy clothes at once, but she never has time even to take care of her own little children. And then she shows me this new finery while I'm working and I'm supposed to look interested and clap my hands and tell her how wonderfully pretty it all is.

"And I'm really so desperately envious. I can barely afford a new cleaning smock. And she goes and suddenly spends more on cocktail things for a single one of their constantly repeated cocktail parties than Ingrid's monthly wages, and that doesn't even include the booze. Not to mention what their dinner parties cost! And the Professor sits at the table and talks about how Sweden's economy is going to be and says he's worried. Out here there's no danger, at least for certain Social Democrats! The rest of us get the most minimal wages. But we're supposed to be friends with her and the Professor, and

be co-workers and say "Du" to each other. To show it
we have to sit with them at the table when Folke
Thunbors and Rickard Sterner are here for Sunday dinner, which I prepared. Fine Social Democrats!"

Then Karna laughed again and ruffled my hair:

"Don't pay any attention to what I just said. It's not
your fault. It's almost time to eat and I just got a little irritated with them and all their nice words today."

Karna was right. I know that now. But they didn't
know what people were saying about their behavior. It
was as if they were blind, I thought. They couldn't see
themselves and couldn't hear themselves talk and therefore didn't know what people really thought of them. I
didn't tell them either. It would just get Karna into trouble. But I had known for a long time how it was. They
were acting. They were false. Their virtue was a sham. I
thought about that now as I stood in front of them in the
big room and Alva changed her voice and spoke ele-
gantly to me as if she were at a podium:

"You can't run away. The real issue is your attitude
toward civic duty and morality. There is a war on now
and that places great demands on all of us. It makes particularly great demands on us in our position. Those who
have had great social advantages must be prepared to
sacrifice personal advantages for the sake of the commu-
nity. You too must take responsibility now that you are
old enough for us to reason with you. You have to show
how smart you really are deep inside. I know I can talk
to you as an adult and that you are worthy of this trust."

But then I protested and said they and their honor

and their party and their position in Sweden were not
the issue. The issue was me and my life. They had
agreed that I should become an immigrant and leave
Sweden for good and now I was, in fact and with their
help, an American with my naturalization papers and
therefore demanded to stay in America. I didn't want to
be sacrificed for their sake. I wanted to stay behind here
in America where I now lived. I said all this to them in
English to prove that I was no longer a Swede, but an
American. I had never before said so much to them so
openly and I knew Gunnar would get angry. I didn't
care about that any more, but told them straight out
exactly what I thought because it was all hopeless anyway.

"I am my own person," I said.

Then Gunnar grabbed me by the neck and shook
me.

"Stop this insolence!" he said.

He held my neck hard, but he didn't let on how
hard because the others were standing around us in a
half circle watching. Alva. Sissela. Kaj. He pretended the
whole thing was a game when he shook me and then
laughed and said:

"Don't be arrogant. Your will needs to grow in the
woods a few more years, my little friend."

He pulled me a little closer and I tried to kick him,
but couldn't reach. His arms were long and he held me
tight by the neck and shook me. He continued to act in
front of Alva and the kids as if it was all a game. I
noticed that and also that his eyes had gone very blue

and he had laugh lines around them. Alva gestured with her hands and the little ones were smiling at him. Kaj, who didn't understand anything because she was too young and couldn't even talk, laughed and clapped her hands.

"See?" he said as he pinned me to the floor. "You can't do anything but flounder. You're still a child and here you'll do as I say."

Sissela, the Little Hypocrite! who understood, began to laugh a high-pitched laugh just as Gunnar had wanted. Alva sighed a little and said what she usually said when it was like this, although this time it was much worse than usual, because they had all heard what I said.

"But, Gunnar, you shouldn't tease Jan."

I tried to kick him again in the shin, but still couldn't reach. He just laughed even more loudly and said:

"I guess I'm stronger than you are. If I say we're going home to Sweden, then there's nothing for you to do but come along."

My mouth had gone completely dry and my whole body cringed and I felt myself beginning to cry from rage because of my powerlessness. That's what he wanted. I knew that. To get me to cry so they could all see it. I made myself cold and rigid and smiled. In this house you didn't cry, not even from anger. I stopped kicking and kept smiling, and very still, bent down with my forehead almost down on the floor and thought as hard as I could without them hearing or seeing anything from me: *"God blast his eyes! God damn him for ever and ever and ever!"*

I didn't say anything they could hear and didn't do anything they could see, but just stood still with bowed head and smiled. Gunnar got tired although Sissela kept on laughing and when he let go after a while I got up. I put my hand up to shade my eyes so I could see outside. It was already night and I could see the Washington Bridge and directly across the Hudson River a neon sign said *THE TIME IS NOW 8:10 P.M.* I saw two big ferry boats. They met out on the river and were completely lit up, and down on the drive the car headlights looked like a string of pearls and I turned around and went into my room.

And now it was all over, now as I stood at the railing, looking in toward New York's Manhattan and knew that everything had come to an end forever. Now the sun had come up. The city rose out of the morning mist as if it were a fairy tale city of pinnacles and towers.

I felt the sun at my neck and it was really morning, but when I turned around I saw I was still all alone on the deck. I stared straight in at the city, held the railing tight and started to form words and speak toward the city. But I did that in a low monotone sing-song voice so no one would be able to really hear what I said if they came up on deck without me noticing and having time to stop. No one would understand and no one would come upon me and what I said was nobody's business but my own.

But now it is the morning when they have all left and I am alone in New York and living my own life and walk toward the station and take the subway to 14th Street down in Lower Manhattan. This is the old New York down here. I walk among all the people between the tall skyscrapers. Nowhere in the whole world do they walk with such assurance as here. The streets are narrow. Only way up high is there sky and sun. There are offices behind all the windows. Now I'm coming to streets where there's almost nothing but antique shops and I look in the windows. There's a wooden Indian, like the ones they used to have in front of cigar stores. He's wearing a feather headdress and everything. I see a small cannon that you light with a lens. It's standing on a bronze platform. There's also a kind of sundial to put in the south window. When the sun reaches its noonday height, the sun comes into focus in the lens and . . . Bang! the whole building knows it's noon. And here I see a big clock from Queen Victoria's time. It's made of iron, like a steam engine from the 1860s, a 2-2-2 with a powerful drive gear and even a clock is built into the locomotive's coal box. I stand there a while and look because in New York you can see the strangest things in shop windows, and then I walk on. Now I'm in the Italian neighborhood, Little Italy as we say in New York. Old Italian men are selling vegetables and fruit and flowers from carts pulled by emaciated horses. Walking here I can see how they hang their wash on lines between the buildings. Black stockings hang in a row beside immaculate ladies' slips and blue panties. Big white sheets hang beside undershirts and the kind of crocheted pads women use for their monthlies. I walk down the narrow street and can barely even see the top stories because of the wash. The wash flutters and flaps between each story. In the small courtyards black-haired girls play hop-scotch. The sun doesn't reach all the way down through these canyons. I walk on and on through the city, past City Hall, and come to Battery Park on the southernmost tip of Manhattan. I walk all the way out and the water laps at the pier under my feet. Beside me I can see the big aquarium where I often go to study sea life. But in front of me as I stand and squint at the sun I see the whole harbor with the Statue of Liberty and all the islands. I see the ferries, passenger ferries and the big ferries that carry whole trains. I see huge ships and intrepid little harbor tugs scamper back and forth. In the far distance I glimpse the MS *Mathilda Thordén* as she heads out. If I try hard maybe I can see through the haze one of the big blue and white Finnish flags painted on the sides to show the U-boats that this is a neutral ship. I wave, but no one can see me from there, so I turn and now I begin walking home up Broadway.

I walk on the left sidewalk uptown. Four cabins were built in 1613 when the white man first settled here and 271 years later, 56 years ago, the first successful skyscraper was built on the same place. No. 52 Broadway was only eight stories tall, and long since torn down. Theobald reported to the class on his research about this very bit of street and its significance. He began with how the ship *Tyger* had burned 326 years before and the captain and crew took refuge here. After that he talked mostly about how No. 52 Broadway showed the world *the feasibility of skeleton steel construction.* Because of this, the long-demolished building was, according to him, more important than the Cunard Building or Standard Oil's huge offices. As I walk I look up at the city and it has become a forest of skyscrapers in the last half-century. I pass the Adams Express Building and there on Wall Street are the great palaces of the banks, the Irving Trust Building and the First National Bank. Inside they sit leaning toward each other across polished desks and plan to enter the European war. I continue walking uptown past the Woolworth Building, which 25 years ago was the tallest in the world at 792 feet. There's no other city in the world like the one where I'm walking home.

But it stopped there because that's not the way it was. It wouldn't have been any better if I had described my walk home as a ticker-tape parade, which I almost thought about doing for awhile. Phtt! It simply wasn't true that I was walking there or could walk there now. It doesn't help to fantasize or say it out loud. It would never be like that again.

Now it was morning and the haze had lifted. The deck was still empty. I turned around and went down to my cabin.

"Now it's all over. Everything," I said.

I lay on my berth and read Mark Twain on the awful German language and laughed so I choked and almost got a stomach cramp.

I had read Mark Twain before but Ralph and Ruth

Bunche had just given me this book. It was 1878 pages long. *The Favorite Works of Mark Twain,* it was called and published last year by the Garden City Publishing Company. And all the pieces included in it were unabridged. *To Jan Myrdal as a memory of America,* Ralph Bunche had written as he gave it to me when they came to the MS *Mathilda Thordén* to say goodbye to Gunnar and Alva.

It wasn't strange that I should laugh. Mark Twain was funny. But the awful German language he made fun of in *The Tale of the Fishwife and Its Sad Fate* was really just the Swedish Swedes spoke in Sweden.

> It is a bleak Day. Hear the Rain, how he pours, and the Hail, how he rattles; and see the Snow, how he drifts along, and oh the Mud, how deep he is! Ah, the poor Fishwife, it is stuck fast in the Mire; it has dropped its Basket of Fishes; and its Hands have been cut by the Scales as it seized some of the falling Creatures; and one Scale has even got into its Eye, and it cannot get her out. It opens its Mouth to cry for Help; but if any Sound comes out of him, alas he is drowned by the raging of the Storm. And now a Tomcat has got one of the Fishes and she will surely escape with him. No, she bites off a Fin, she holds her in her Mouth,—will she swallow her? No, the Fishwife's brave Mother-Dog deserts his Puppies and rescues the Fin,—which he eats, himself, as his Reward.

That's why Germans and Swedes could never understand that we in America and other countries have to laugh until we choke when we see phrases like this in the middle of the printed page:

ALTHERTHUMSWISSENSSCHAFTEN.
KINDERBEWAHRUNGSANSTALTEN.
UNABHAENGIGKEITSERKLAERUNGEN.
WAFFENSTILLSTANDSUNTERHANDLUNGEN.

Studies of ancient civilizations.
Child care centers.
Declarations of independence.
Disarmament negotiations.

VAPENSTILLESTÅNDSFÖRHANDLINGAR.
OAVHANGIGHETSFÖRKLARINGAR.
BARNUPPFOSTRINGSANSTALTER.
FORNTIDSVETENSKAPER.

Armisticenegotiations.
Independencedelarations.
Childrearingcenters.
Classicagestudies.

Has det varit på västkusten i år?

Is it to have been on the West Coast this year?

Would Madame Assistantcrownmarshall like a lump of sugar or would she like another cup of coffee?

FÄLTMARSKALKSUNIFORMSPERSEDEL.
LOKFÖRARBITRÄDESMÖSSA.
KONSUMENTKOOPERATIONSIDEAL.

Fieldmarshalluniformaccessory.
Assistantrailroadengineer'scap.
Consumercooperationideal.

It could get still worse. Just make possessives out of the words by changing the endings!

KONSUMENTKOOPERATIONSIDEALEN.
LOKFÖRARBITRÄDESMÖSSORNA.
FÄLTMARSKALKUNIFORMSPERSEDLARNAS.

The ideal of consumer cooperation.
Assistant railroad engineer's cap.
Accessories to field marshall uniforms.

I tried various Swedish words and expressions there as I lay in my berth with the big book on my stomach and I laughed so I choked, time after time. Out there they pounded on the door, but I paid no attention. I didn't answer. I just lay and laughed.

CHAPTER 2

The city outside the walls now was Stockholm, and I just smiled. The streetcars down on the square were blue. I saw them inside myself because I couldn't see them through the window from where I sat. I couldn't get up and go to the window either. I sat in a row with them; Gunnar and Alva and Sissela and Kaj, against the inner wall here in the hotel room above Norrmalmstorg where the Myrdal family was holding its first press conference since coming home.

Blue streetcars rumbling along, rattling along and a pink trip slip for a three cent fare. Everything out there on the other side of the window looked like itself, but now there were sandbags outside the MEA department store show window. Maybe a bomb attack was coming. Sirens would wail through the night. Now the streets were full of people seeking shelter. Gray-haired ladies swung their umbrellas around so they could be first in line for the bomb shelter. The steel doors closed. Boom! it would say and there would be only gravel left of the building. Boom! and the NK department store, biggest in Scandinavia, disappeared too. *I'm going to blow that place to kingdom come, he muttered and looked scowlingly through the bombsights at NK.* Now the bombs were screaming.

Weak blue light from blackout lamps. Later in the middle of the night it would be completely dark in the streets and squares when the power plant blew up. And in all the houses all over town, people would shit in their bathtubs this winter because the waterworks were closed and all the sewers were plugged up and there were no toilets and everything froze anyway, but it began to smell when spring came. That's what they did in Petsamo at the Arctic Ocean. And the bodies had just been buried. And this was actually a small town. *A small town in the old world.* It wasn't a real town, not like Chicago or New York or even the Twin Cities, St. Paul and Minneapolis, so you could get away from it fast if you wanted to escape. The big battleships were riding their anchors out in the harbor, they dreaded nought and their guns were thundering towards the city, and building after building fell down and people rolled around in the streets and died and black hearses rocked, and clattered over the cobblestones. Bombers came wave after wave again and finally there was nothing that could tell the traveller passing by a hundred years later where the Swedes' Stockholm had stood.

But I didn't let anyone know that I thought like this. It was harmless for me to think this way, even though they were in the room looking straight at me. No one could get out of me what I was thinking to myself, no matter how they tried. I just sat quietly and smiled and made my eyes blank behind my glasses with gold frames, as they were called even though it was only gold-colored metal. It was the Stockholm Hotel high above Norrmalmstorg on Monday afternoon, May 27, 1940, and Alva and Gunnar met the press with their children beside them.

They had come to Stockholm from New York and were going to be interviewed. On the MS *Mathilda Thordén* we had gone north up between Greenland and Iceland to continue northeast on the Arctic Ocean above the North Cape towards the Finnish port, Petsamo. We went that way because we didn't have safe conduct. But we hadn't come to Stockholm on a boat or train. Per Albin saw to it that the government picked us up with a plane, a Junkers, from a military airport at Petsamo. Young Finnish recruits practiced throwing hand grenades before war came; they all talked about it. When they practiced sharpshooting they shot at a Russian Red Army helmet.

"Hit the star!"

"Don't tell anyone about this," Alva said, but I didn't know if she knew I had a helmet like that packed away to take along.

We couldn't talk about the columns of Swedish cars up there at Petsamo or how the sacks of sugar in the warehouse at the pier broke open and there was a river of sweet sludge running through the mud toward the water. There hadn't been time to take it away. War materiel, cannons, boxes of ammunition, barrels of explosives, and all of that was being transported south in cars. She forbade me to say anything about what it was like to visit the last Norwegian fighting unit. But there wasn't anything special to tell.

We were pulled across the river by a little ferry which ground forward and could barely hold a truck and

there among the stunted birches on the other shore was
Norway and lost Norwegians stood there in their uniforms. A thin-haired Norwegian captain, whom Gunnar
thought he knew from a conference in Oslo in the summer of 1935, believed the war would be over soon now.
The Finnish major who took charge of us said later, after
we had come back:

"They'll give up soon."

And I knew that already because from the MS
Mathilda Thordén at night I had seen a British convoy
on its way out as we passed northern Norway. The steward woke me up and asked me to come up on deck and
look. The British were taking home their forces because
Hitler's Panzers were going through Holland and
Belgium like a warm knife through butter, he said. It was
probably because they thought it was all over up here
that neither the German U-boat off North Cape nor the
two Russian vessels off Petsamo paid any attention to us.
They didn't even ask to see our papers.

If I had been a Norwegian general I would have set
an example by having any captain shot if he said it was
over. When you looked at the map you could see that if
the Norwegians only wanted to, they could defend themselves up there even if the English and French did go
home. They lack perseverance. The major was right
about that. I had drawn the whole thing with red and
blue arrows on the map while we were flying to
Stockholm.

But I hadn't told anyone about it. And I wasn't
going to say anything now either. I put down my pen

and looked up from the map when they led him in. He was the bad apple in the basket. This put me face to face with a duty I couldn't escape. It was a difficult thing to bear sole responsibility for everyone's well-being. With a tired gesture I took off my glasses and stroked my close-cropped graying hair. As brigadier with responsibility for the whole front, I hadn't slept in three days now that the British had left. Here in the command post buried deep under the earth the kerosene lamp swung listlessly and the bombardment continued. The captain had been handcuffed. He started to make a statement, but I interrupted him:

"Maybe he doesn't know about it or even mean it, but he's a traitor!" I said to Corporal Felton, who was chief of the guard force. "He is as shrewd as Milady! Don't let him talk you into anything. Shoot him at dawn in front of all the men!"

I handed over the order I had signed for the good of the country and the prisoner was led out.

This would strengthen fighting morale, I knew. Now the men outside cheered at the news. They were relieved that the staff had been purged of the doubting and that the fifth column had been unmasked. The operation against the German troops could begin. The orderly brought in a fresh steaming pot of hot black coffee. The Germans had brought out their Howitzers.

"They've started to shoot real seriously," I said when the dugout shook and earth fell from the ceiling so I had to wipe out the coffee cup with a handkerchief before I filled it up.

"Yes, sir, General." said the orderly.

I drank three more cups of coffee. Then I got up out of the chair, put on my Sam Brown belt and walked the muddy passage through the old trench. The rest of the day I inspected the troops on their way to the front. My plan was carefully worked out, taking the geography into consideration. The Germans were already exhausted after the fighting around Narvik and now they would be trapped, as if in pincers. It was a cool day with a breeze over the tundra.

"Synchronize your watches with mine," I said to the officers. "The time is now precisely eleven forty-five zero zero."

Then I turned to the American war correspondent and said:

"Zero hour is three forty-five a.m. tomorrow. Then we go over the top."

They could have done something like that if they had wanted to. Only for real, of course.

Here at the hotel, the reporters sat and looked at me. It hadn't been necessary to warn me, I didn't intend to say anything anyway. Nothing about what I saw in Petsamo or what I had fantasized.

I would have been able to talk to Nelson about what I had seen, and a little more too, but who could I talk to here? As far as fantasies were concerned, I had sometimes been able to tell Karna a few things last year. I had lain on the red rug in front of her bed and talked to her when she had stayed at home even though it was her free evening, or sat up on the bench at the kitchen window while she worked. I didn't tell her everything, of course. Especially not about her. And I wouldn't have talked about Barbara, who was now our music and folkways teacher, even if Karna had still been around. Not only was her name Barbara, but she looked a little bit daring and smart like Barbara Stanwyck and I saw her at night sometimes in my dreams, sort of like Stella. I had talked to Karna about the girls we were going to get to come with us to the observation deck high up over the Riverside Drive Viaduct, at 125th Street. She asked me more about that and smiled a little, but the tales I told myself about her at night, I couldn't even think about when she was in the next room. She listened to what I said and she laughed sometimes too, but not nastily, and she never said anything to anyone—not even Ingrid—about what I told her. She talked and laughed a lot herself and could tell really dirty Kålle and Ada stories when she felt like it. She had gone home to Sweden on the SS *Stavanger* when the war started and then she got a kidney inflammation in the fall. Since then I hadn't found anyone I could talk to about things like that. I didn't talk at all with the Irishwoman in the kitchen and had kept everything to myself. And what could I tell Alva and Gunnar? I didn't talk to them about anything anymore and they never knew about my fantasies. Not for many years anyway. Not since I had learned how to build fantasies.

They didn't understand such things. That you could lie on your back on the carpet, silent and still, with eyes open and just think and tell stories and see things in your mind. Gunnar got angry and said I was lazy when he found me last spring on the carpet, fantasizing in front of the fire. But it wasn't a fire, only electrical lamps behind synthetic logs. Lazy and fat. He told me we came from a family of hardworking farmers and that by much slothfulness the building decayeth; and through idleness of the hands the house droppeth through.

They didn't even understand that I was thinking about what I read, although they had seen me read. I had tried to talk to Gunnar about this once last winter, it must have been in the middle of February. He was home in New York and it was Sunday. The Sterners were there and we were all eating in the dining room. Gunnar seemed to be in good humor. He had been down South and talked about how even a very well-known economist at a university had seriously believed in the *black baby myth*. A woman who had slept with a black man once could suddenly, years later, give birth to a black baby, after living monogamously and faithfully in a marriage with a white man. It had happened at the university with a colleague's wife. Weeping, she confessed that when she was sixteen their black gardener had seduced her. It was a real *rape,* she said. Now she was 33 and the punishment had come. And the professor believed this!

"He became totally unreasonable when I pointed out that this contradicted basic genetics," said Gunnar. "So deep in the subconscious are the roots of racial prejudice."

When he was in a good mood and there were guests present, Gunnar would often tell fascinating stories like this. I had also read them in what he wrote. His were as interesting as other books. When he was quiet for a moment at the table I began to talk about something I had been thinking about, which was connected with my schoolwork.

It was a question of reason and logic, as I had said when I told Miss Evans about my discussion with Mr. Flourens. He and I had talked about the history of the steam engine and the significance of idleness for mankind while I was in the library reading. I had said nothing about him, of course. He was secretive. She had listened to me and then said I was a little philosopher.

"You are quite the philosopher," she had said, and Mr. Flourens would have said the last word in French.

"But," I now said at the lunch table and turned to Gunnar, "if you think about it, isn't laziness really the origin of all invention and progress?"

To explain what I meant I told Gunnar and everyone at the table about a 12-year-old other than myself. I talked about Humphrey Potter, who in 1713 was operating a Newcomen steam machine. At every stroke the valves had to be opened and closed by hand. But Humphrey Potter found the work hard, he was lazy and because of that he saw the connection between the work he had been assigned to do and the movement of the balance arm on the machine. One valve should be open when the arm was down and the valve would begin to close as the arm lifted and the other valve would work the other way around. If he were inattentive and dull the machine slowed down and if he made a mistake he could cause a catastrophe. Because the work was boring and Humphrey Potter preferred to go outside and play, he tied a cord to the balance arm and it opened and closed the valves as the balance arm moved. Laziness showed the way! The machine could now take care of itself. The invention was perfected in 1718 by Beighton and became the *plug-frame* which made the Newcomen machine more effective.

"Actually it was Pantin's safety valve for his *new digester*, his steam pressure cooker of 1681, and Humphrey Potter's discovery that the Newcomen machine could operate itself, which laid the groundwork for the industrial revolution," I said. "And so the leap was made from tool to machine. In both cases laziness led them to their discoveries."

But I didn't really get to say this last bit because Gunnar interrupted me and told me to be quiet. Before I even got to the conclusion, the industrial revolution. He turned to Rickard Sterner, laughed and said:

"The boy sounds really learned."

Then everyone else at the table laughed too and began talking about something else. I had intended to talk about Watt too, who became such a great inventor just because his head wasn't full of recognized truths and other bad school knowledge; he looked for himself. Actually the whole World's Fair, *The World of Tomorrow*, was about this. There were descriptions of how people had been freed more and more from *drudgery* in the 150 years since 1789. But now I was glad I hadn't been able to say more about what I had been thinking. None of them wanted to respond to me and discuss and I was embarrassed that I had said anything at all about it to them. I stamped on my own foot to remind myself never to do that again. As I sat quietly at the table I thought— fantasized—that it was the year before and I was sitting in Karna's room, telling her everything. The story about Denis Papin and the technical meaning for the industrial revolution of his so-called new food digester particularly interested her. She said she had read about it herself in her course, but in a different context. She was studying dietetics and did experiments on white mice and about how many calories various activities required. Then she certainly had read too about the *new digester*, which was the first new cooking device invented since ancient times. I could fantasize that way too. That I was talking to someone I knew and that they answered me as if it were for real. Like when I fantasized about talking to Karna about Papin. When I talked with them like that I gradually slipped into letting them come forth and began visualizing them, especially Karna. But I didn't want to think that through except when I was all alone and it was dark.

It wasn't strange that I didn't say anything to Alva about the fantasizing. She would only have asked a lot of questions and made notes and leaned her head toward me like a bird and look at me with pursed lips and ask me to explain in more detail whether I had said you could look and make something happen with what you saw, partly controlling it, but not entirely. How is that? Explain! What are you thinking about? Say more!

Do you see anything? What do you mean by that? She had done that when I was smaller and hadn't learned to hold my tongue.

She had heard about fantasizing. She had given lectures about children's fantasies when she was Director of the Social Pedagogical Institute and now she was studying that at the university. Several of the books she was reading about hypnagogic hallucinations and eidetic imaging and whatever else it was were interesting. Especially the case histories. One was about adolescent girls and their fantasies. First I read through it and then I took it to my room and read the exciting parts about girls' masturbation fantasies time after time. But she couldn't have really understood this book either. What she read was just words for her. She didn't understand any of it. She couldn't fantasize! She wasn't able to visualize things in this way and didn't know what it was like to bring up these images. Karna knew without having to ask. They were different in every other way too. Alva couldn't laugh spontaneously like Karna either. She couldn't stand naturally, she assumed a standing position, I had once told Karna when I watched through the window in the kitchen door how Alva greeted visitors.

"You shouldn't say that about your mother," Karna had said.

But she laughed too. That Alva was one way and Karna another was not because Alva was a professional woman and an intellectual. Karna worked much harder than Alva and she went to Columbia University and read in the evenings and on her days off.

"Today is Blue Monday," said Karna.

She had gone to a dance at Columbia's International House the night before. I knew she had come home late and understood what she meant. I was home because I had a cold. But that was just what I told Alva as she was on her way out and happened to see I was home. I had started to read Edward Hungerford's railroad book *Pathway of Empire* the evening before and stayed home from school to finish it. Karna knew I wasn't sick, but she didn't tell Alva. When Alva had gone, she laughed and said:

"Today is Blue Monday."

She was cutting a bright yellow grapefruit section by section. But if I took her literally, Mondays weren't blue. They were green in a way. Thursdays were blue. Fridays were yellow.

"Sundays are red," said Karna. "Can you see that when you think about it?"

I was sitting on the bench with the sun at my back. I looked at her bent over the fruit and she understood me when I said that February was out to the right and descended while June came up from below and stretched itself to the left toward July. She also thought that if you looked from the year 1800 back at 1799, it was like time turned a corner and ran down to the 1600s and further down. But if you looked at 1776, it was up on a shelf to the left and time ran in the opposite direction down toward Napoleon. I had never told anyone about these things before and while I talked I looked at her neck. The sunshine glittered on the short blonde down on her arms as she cut and suddenly my eyes followed the line of her hip. Her body moved a little under the light blue dress as she stood and I couldn't resist. My eyes followed the line down from her hips. The dress was tight on her thigh when she took a half step. I could see her knee in the gap where the fabric strained against the buttons holding the skirt together. Her suntanned legs were bare and she was wearing white tennis socks. I noticed I was blushing. I didn't want her to see me, so I jumped down from the bench and rushed to my room.

I swallowed. I held my lips together and swallowed. There had been sunshine on Karna's hair in front of me and I watched as she cut out section after section. I didn't want to see that when other people were around and I said no! no! no! silently to myself to change my thoughts. That was last fall and it was in New York and now it was May in Stockholm and the reporters were gathered and there sat the whole Myrdal family on exhibit: Gunnar, Alva, Sissela, and Kaj. I sat there too beside them, smiling. I had been called to the press conference from the hotel room. First they sent a maid after me. But she couldn't get me out of the room. I was reading, I said, and I was too. I said that politely because it wasn't her fault they had sent her to get me. I had taken Walter Scott's *Quentin Durward* from my jacket pocket and began to read it again during the last hour in the plane from Petsamo. Then Alva came and tried to talk to me. I could hear she wanted to coax me:

"It doesn't look right if you're not there!"

But she couldn't get me out either. She didn't even

get the door open. Even though it was unlocked. She didn't control me any more. I had known she would be sent to get me out when the maid was unsuccessful. I had put the book aside, open on the night table, and placed myself ready at the unlocked door.

They hadn't let me have a key to the hotel room precisely so I wouldn't be able to lock myself in. Ever since I had begun locking myself in so I could get some peace, they had always taken the key away as soon as we arrived in a new place. On the boat they hadn't been able to do that. You could lock the door from the inside so they would have had to order a special key to open it up if they wanted to break in. They didn't want to do that. They contented themselves with talking and chirping and then pounding and tugging because they were reluctant to have other people see how it was in the family. If I were going to be locked in, they would do the locking. That's how it had been with them as long as I could remember.

I waited for her. Listened for the steps. There was no hitting in our family, they used to say, and talk about how children had been beaten in the past. What Gunnar did when he got angry wasn't called hitting. The family just said he was irritated. Gunnar didn't strike me with his belt, as Olle said his father did with him, or with the cane, as he said he himself had been beaten in school, or punch me with his fist or anything. When he got really angry he had a hard time not boxing my ears. Alva chirped extra high then.

I could tell the reporters about it:

"Our family isn't old-fashioned, it's modern and pedagogically it follows a clearly behavioristic method of child-rearing, including a tested and psychologically scientific graded scale of punishments for children."

All the reporters would jump if I said that. They wouldn't believe their ears. Alva would purse her lips and Gunnar would pretend I was joking. But that's how it was. Kaj was too little to punish, she couldn't speak very well yet and so didn't understand. Sissela didn't need to be punished. She understood so well, Gunnar thought. It would be justified, though, to punish me after a proper discussion in which I had the right to defend myself with correctly formed logical arguments. But when I was able to do that and learned to answer them in their own way, they said I was a sophist. Then there was a serious family meeting about morals and responsibility and respect for norms. The intention was that I should respond by saying I understood how right they were. If I didn't do that, fines were deducted from my weekly allowance.

In earlier years they used to send me away from the table without dessert if something happened while I was at the table or sentence me to be locked in if it was serious. As if that would bother me now! When I was little, though, I was afraid of the dark and of being locked in the dark. When the door to the closet was closed and I heard the key turn, the dark was icy around me and it went up my back and my throat stuck together. If I let them hear I was afraid and started to cry I got to come out. If I asked forgiveness they stroked my hair and said they felt sorry for me and understood me, but wanted the best for me and that I must understand that because we all loved each other and always told each other the truth and I got to come back to the table and eat my dessert. Afterward the shame felt sticky all over my body. I still remembered that with nauseated discomfort as I stood inside the door waiting for Alva to come through the corridor to fetch me.

It had been a long time now since I had been locked in the dark, before we went to America, because the shame had been so horrible that I had forced myself to look straight into the darkness and through the darkness and so learned the dark. I could see what I wanted and think what I wanted and then they couldn't get to me at all. They could lock me in if they wanted. When they realized I had stopped being afraid they didn't want to lock me in anymore. They forbade me to lock myself in instead. We were going to be a modern, open free family in which we talked about everything with each other. But I got myself a key to my closet door. They didn't notice that. I think.

So I didn't get to have a key to the hotel room. But even though the door couldn't be locked, Alva hadn't been able to get it open when she came through the corridor and took hold of the doorknob. For more than a year I had been stronger than she was and as soon as I heard her approach I braced my foot against the door and held it hard when she pulled at it. I was completely silent. I didn't answer her with a single word no matter what she said. The door had to stay closed. I tried to breathe so quietly that she wouldn't hear breathing either, although I had to exert myself to hold the door when she pulled. But then came Gunnar and he was stronger than I. He opened the door with a single tug and took me by the neck and shook me.

"Don't kick and don't talk back! Just come along! And look happy!"

Then he laughed so his teeth sparkled when he held me by the neck and pushed me in front of him through the hotel corridor.

"Keep smiling!" he said.

When we entered the press conference ("Here we are—Janne and I," Gunnar said boyishly) we both smiled at the reporters because we were a famous family and a modern intellectual family about whom much had been written. The Myrdals were mentioned in all the weekly papers and everything printed about them was cut out and saved. Alva and Gunnar were known for being young and successful and happy and in love and to be living in a companionate marriage, so they always called each other *darling* when a reporter was listening and it was shameful that I was the way I was and I was fat too and nearsighted because the whole family was supposed to be successful and happy and athletic.

Now I sat there in the same room with the family and smiled the whole time and looked straight ahead through the reporters so they were flat and colorless like old photographs, blurred if I wanted and clear if I wanted, while I sang to myself. It was almost like a chant:

Punch, brothers! Punch with care!
Punch in the presence of the passenjare!
A pink trip slip for a three cent fare!

I was looking at Alva now because she was talking. She held her head in a half profile toward the reporters, as usual. I know she thought that was her best side for pictures:

"If other Swedish children, yes, millions of children in Europe, can be exposed to danger, ours can too."

The reporters took notes. One of them, a woman with gray streaked hair and a gray suit, sighed and said:

"If only all mothers could be so principled and self-less!"

Alva nodded at her, cool, well-groomed and blonde, and continued to speak:

"I think that if a small group of people in a country are persecuted, they have a right to flee and seek asylum. But if a whole country is threatened with misfortune, then the individual must not seek to save himself, while others, the whole population, have to stay where they are."

She was wearing her dark-blue suit. The one she had bought at Macy's the day before we got on board to leave America. It was more modern than anything they had in Sweden.

An older reporter with horn-rimmed glasses in a dark suit and black bow-tie said thoughtfully:

"Many people are coming to Sweden from down on the Continent, where there is war. Both those who are really in distress, as you say, Professor. But there are also the others you have mentioned. Those who call themselves refugees so they can come to Sweden and live here among us, but who are really just deserting their own people. They're trying to save their own skins in an egotistical way."

"That is why it wouldn't be right for us to make exceptions for our own children," said Alva.

"We come from Swedish peasant stock," said Gunnar. "That's what I told my son when he asked to stay behind at his school in America. We aren't like British aristocrats who sent boatloads of their children to safety in America when it got difficult and dangerous for people in their own country."

Then he talked about his work on the race problem in America. He would return to his work there as soon as possible.

"You have to finish what you begin, no matter what the world situation may be, and when things are calm here at home I will, of course, return at once to my great task in America. One shouldn't leave a job half done. For now, I have left research assistant Sterner of the Social Administration and his wife to carry on the work. He'll be there in my place to supervise everything. The race problem in North America is, in fact, much more than a race issue. It is a question of the whole American society and the democratic tradition. I have decided to write a groundbreaking work. I am working on a project like the one de Tocqueville did exactly one hundred years ago. One must never forget what is owed to the great pioneers. I have a wider view than de Tocqueville because I stand on his shoulders. What I'm writing now is intended to be the twentieth century's *De la démocratie en Amérique.*"

Gunnar took off his hat. It was warm in the room and he tossed his head to get his forelock free, the one reporters described as "unruly" in the clippings Alva had me paste before when I needed money.

"Is de Tocqueville still an important name in the American debate?" asked a blond thirty-year-old reporter in gray flannel pants and blue jacket. His hair was thin and straggling and shining with hair oil, I saw. If you touched him and stroked him like you do with a dog, you would have greasy hands afterward. Karna used to say that no girl with any common sense would let a guy like that into her room because he would leave tracks behind him.

"Sort of like a snail."

And if he bent down and put his head on the ground, locked his hands behind his neck and walked backward on his elbows and knees through the room with his bottom sticking up in the air and head down so he dragged his hair across the hotel room's green rug, there would be a shiny dark snail track.

"The debate about the nature of democracy in a state with a representative government under a constitution and laws remains central in an America which we all know is the greatest stronghold of Western democracy and civilization," answered Gunnar.

I wondered if any of the reporters would notice

there was no more talk about peasant heritage and staying in the homeland. Gunnar had changed the direction
of what he was telling them and now he said he would
go back to America as soon as possible. But no one
seemed to notice anything. Gunnar was talking about
Roosevelt now and what he meant to America with his
brain trust, the young intellectual New Deal generation
which had lifted democracy out of the apathy of the
twenties and now for two terms had had the opportunity
to affect social development with practical policies from
the command positions the president in Washington gave
them.

"In the United States, this is a victory for reasoned
social common sense, for a policy of the middle way,"
he said. "It is no coincidence that not only Keynes and
theories in general, but also Swedish practice and
Sweden's experience with a modern crisis policy, yes,
Scandinavia's experience as a whole, have stood in
recent years at the center of the insightful social debate
over there and we do not need to be ashamed to
remember that our example, therefore, means something
in the renewal."

"Do you mean, Professor, that we have inspired
Roosevelt to new ways of thinking?" said the one with
the oiled hair.

"That would be boasting," said Gunnar. "After all,
Sweden is a very small frog in a big pond and we must
not puff ourselves up so much that we are unnecessarily
conspicuous."

Everyone laughed. Whatever the reporters say when

they ask questions and whatever they write later in their newspapers, no one, not even Alva and Gunnar, can know what they're thinking to themselves deep inside as they sit here. I continued to smile the whole time and maybe they wrote in their notebooks in very small handwriting way down on the side that Gunnar really just said that there had once been a *blue trip slip for an eight cent trip!*

Now that Gunnar was quiet, Sissela spoke. Gunnar and Alva nodded encouragingly at her as she stood up and spoke to the press. Her voice was almost like Alva's, only smaller, of course. She was not quite six years old now. But she was the one of us children who spoke when we met reporters. Gunnar kept his hand on my shoulder, warning. I knew what would happen later, afterward, if I started talking to reporters and said straight out what Gunnar and Alva thought I was going to say if I got the chance, so I just continued to smile.

"This country is so clean," said Sissela. "There isn't as much garbage and dirt all over as there is in America."

Alva laughed. It rang through the room. I heard she had taken out her rippling laugh.

"Yes, the girl said exactly that as soon as she got to Sweden and looked out the window and saw the spring-green farmland and the blue May sky. Swedish cleanliness was the first thing she remarked on when she saw Sweden. She was so small when we left that she hardly remembers anything from here."

"Sweden is so clean and pretty," said Sissela. "Swedes don't throw their garbage on the neighbor's property.

Instead, they help each other keep things clean."

She stood quiet for a moment. It was as if she was searching for words. The reporters nodded encouragingly at her.

"And the cottages are red too," she added in a clear voice and looked straight ahead.

"That's what you told your mother on the train when you looked out the compartment window somewhere after Haparanda and saw Sweden for the first time," said the female reporter and tilted her head at an angle as ladies liked to do when they talked with Sissela.

"Yes, the country was green and pretty," said Sissela and her voice was very clear and light as she said it. The reporters obviously didn't know the government had picked us up with a plane. Sissela understood without being told that she shouldn't say anything about that, although it was not one of all those things Alva had told us to remember not to say or to pretend we didn't know. That was why Sissela went along with the idea that we had come on the train.

I turned my head and looked at her. She stood up straight and looked directly at the reporters with her large clear little-girl eyes. When I looked at them again they sat there writing. They showed no sign of disbelief. Maybe they were not thinking something entirely different deep inside after all. Maybe they were thinking what they wrote. They believed her! They could just as well have believed Shirley Temple! They didn't even react to the mention of red cottages up north. As if they hadn't read about Sweden in the elementary school reading book and knew that cottages in the north were gray, like in Finland and Russia!

Sissela had not seen any red cottages in the taxi cab from Bromma airport in to Norrmalmstorg, I thought. She's just talking about what she's seen in picture books Alva showed her. And if the reporters don't notice something strange about all this, they are just as dumb and gullible as Gunnar always said newspaper people are.

And no one had asked what Gunnar was actually going to do here in Sweden and why he had come here. The reporters just listened and took notes when Alva talked about ethics and Gunnar about peasant heritage and things like that. I would have liked to hear Gunnar's answer to that question. He had said nothing about it to me, not so that I heard, anyway. Had Per Albin called him home to Sweden? And, if so, why? Were the Germans allowing him to work here? Sweden was, after all, a little Germany. Everyone in New York knew that now and there were German soldiers in Denmark and Norway and the Germans were winning the war and Hitler didn't like Gunnar. And he had flicked cherry pits at the Storm Troopers' boots and had a lot of trouble with that when when he was in Germany before the war. Gunnar had told Markelius about it when the World's Fair opened. So they probably didn't want him in Sweden. And now Gunnar had talked about going back to America. How did that fit together? The reporters' bosses maybe didn't allow them to ask questions like that. It wasn't like it was with us in America, where reporters questioned and questioned and didn't just nod and make notes.

Alva was still sitting smiling in half profile beside Sissela, who stood gazing with clear eyes. Little Hypocrite! But that is what I would have been if they had got what they wanted. They had wanted a son who was like them and they got me instead. That was probably the reason Alva wept so much after the miscarriage in June the year before. She didn't think I knew. She started to bleed before she reached the hospital. It was her third miscarriage and this time too it had been a boy.

"It's like a curse," she had said to Gunnar when she came home from the hospital. "It is as if there were a curse on us. It's like we can't have a real son. Only girls."

"And Jan, of course," she added.

"Yes, Jan," said Gunnar.

Then they were quiet. After a while she wept again. They didn't think I was home. But I sure was home, I heard them. And I knew what they meant. Sissela couldn't carry on the name, she was a girl. The one they had been expecting now was like the second miscarriage. He would have been called Thomas or Peter and be musical, like Gunnar. Now it was too late.

"I don't think I can do it one more time," said Alva.

It didn't matter that I had heard them talk about that last year. I had known how it was as long as I could remember. And maybe it was a sad thing for them.

Now we were all being photographed. Gunnar still had his hand on my shoulder and he did things with his eyes and forelock the way he did when he knew there were photographers in the room and he saw camera lenses pointed at him. Several pictures were taken. Gunnar put his hat on. It had an American shape; as if he were playing William Powell without a mustache. I smiled into the camera, smiled and smiled and smiled.

"A buff trip slip for a six cent fare!"

I took the whole rhyme from the beginning again: I told the whole story one more time but didn't move my mouth and didn't even blink. But I opened my unblinking eyes a little wider, strained them and stared from behind my glasses at all of them. If it had been two thousand years ago and this had been Greece, everyone in the room would have been turned to stone forever by such eyes.

No one knew what I was thinking as I sat there and smiled and never, never, never again would a photographer photograph me together with them and their family. And never, never, never again would I participate in one of this family's press conferences.

CHAPTER 3

I sat in the window recess and waited. I chewed on peanuts and had already been waiting twenty minutes. They were going to live at the Petersen house on Munkbron now that they were home. They had rented it for the summer from a diplomat who had been transferred. Beside me on the deep windowseat was a large round gray-green cactus in a black glazed pot. The cactus was shaped almost like a ball. By the door was another cactus in a black glazed pot on a white lacquer shelf that looked like a step. It was one of those sprawling cactuses with tall arms and long nasty spikes. Sort of like a Swedish Christmas candlestick. Only dusty green. On a white shag rug in the middle of the floor stood a large glass table with brass legs. On it was a large glass bowl almost full of peanuts. There were bunches of grapes and human figures engraved in the surface of the glass under the peanuts. I could see girls' arms that stuck up and some legs. And beside the peanut bowl was a heavy rectangular ashtray of almost transparent glass with something like gold veins. There were no butts in the ashtray, but it hadn't been washed either. The help hadn't been here to clean for them. When they went to bed they probably just emptied the butts into the brass wastebasket over there under the white lacquer telephone table. But I didn't go over there to look. On the black tea cart stood a white porcelain bowl in the shape of a big grape leaf. There had been four green olives, which I had already eaten. An Isaac Grünewald hung on the short wall above the Aalto bentwood chair. There was another Aalto chair beside the low bar cabinet in light birch. Its glass top had been pulled out. It wasn't dry yet. The glasses were gone but the rings they made were still there. Some of the rings were small and dried red. Others were larger and still sort of sticky when I looked at them.

Gunnar had probably served eggnog. He used to do that because he liked sweet things like that. Just like he liked cloudberry preserves and cherry liqueur and punch. He had cloudberry preserves in a jar in the desk drawer on Riverside Drive too, next to a package of small sugared rusks. He used to scoop up a little of the preserves with the rusk to chew on while he sat reading and he also had a small silver cup with cherry liqueur beside him when he sat writing. Karna had laughed about it. But we couldn't let on that we knew. He got furious if he discovered I'd been nibbling at his preserves. No one else was allowed to eat the cloudberry preserves. It was so hard to get hold of here in America, he thought, and Markelius had arranged to have jars of preserves sent to him special from Sweden. Cloudberries were the only thing he really liked, so it was right that he should have them for himself. But I used to sample his preserves anyway, with the small sugar rusks. It did no good to lock them up. I had duplicate keys to their locks and besides, you can always open desk drawer locks like that with a knife or a safety pin. It wasn't only

Gunnar who liked cloudberry preserves. I liked
cloudberry preserves too. In Alaska we in America had a
kind of cloudberry, salmonberries, but only the Eskimos
used them. They put them up for the winter in seal oil
and eat them to prevent scurvy. I heard that in school.
Then I had told how they make cloudberry sauce in
Norway and Sweden and Finland with cloudberries and
water. And I was the only one in my class who had
eaten cloudberry preserves.

There was a straight white vase with white sirens on
the bar. It was reflected in the long frameless mirror on
the wall behind. The sirens had started to fade, though.
On the little white telephone table was a brown envelope. In the Grünewald picture some women were dancing. It was ornate, the way his paintings were. They
liked Grünewald. I didn't. I liked Matisse instead and had
seen the red girls dancing on green grass against a blue
sky by Matisse when the museum at home in New York
had celebrated its tenth anniversary. On the wall with
the window in my room on Riverside Drive I had had a
Matisse print I bought at the museum when I was there.
It was a colorful picture with lots of red in it of a girl
lying on a sofa with flowers beside her. She scratched
her hair and was naked, but no one said anything about
me having her on the wall because it was a Matisse and
besides she was naked in an artistic way so you couldn't
really see her. There was another picture which I had
not dared to buy because they would have said something about it even if it was a Matisse. A girl was partway
on her back with her hands over her head and her body

sort of turned forward. Matisse wasn't bad. I liked the
painting the French had in their pavilion at the World's
Fair better. It was a Degas. And Renoir, too, of course.
Maybe I liked him even better than anyone else who
painted girls. But I had wondered if the reading girl in
the red chair at the World's Fair really had a dress like
that or if the painter had pulled it down over her left
shoulder to show more of her breast. He had painted her
from a little above too. Maybe it wasn't a dress, but a
nightgown. But if she had stood up straight it would
have fallen off her. It was a nice painting.

In any case, Matisse was much better than
Grünewald who was famous only in Sweden, a local
Swedish painter, just an imitator. A little limp and sloppy.
But he was one of their friends and they went to the
same parties, so they got upset when I said he was nothing special and they told me I was talking nonsense and
he was a significant painter. Gunnar got really angry
then too, raging as if I had taken some of his cloudberry
preserves, and told me to shut up and not to talk about
things I didn't understand.

I knew what I liked. I liked Salvador Dali, for example. You could see exactly what he had painted, the lines
didn't vibrate. What you saw in his pictures was very
clear. Like a day with no fog at all. But still, everything
was completely different. Like you had wandered into a
dream. And at the same time it was funny. He was
inventive. The clocks on the post card I bought for ten
cents at the museum, for example, that bent over bushes
and corners and the dead horse and all that. He was like

Gunnar Ekelöf in *Late Arrival on Earth,* which I had
taken when they cleaned out the bookshelves in
Bromma and which I used to read aloud to Karna:

> crush the alphabet between your teeth yawn
> vowels, the fire is burning in hell vomit and spit
> now or never I and dizziness you or never dizzi-
> ness now or never.
>   we begin again
>   crush the alphabet macadam and your teeth
> yawn vowels . . .

I rolled the R and opened the A and sharpened the
S and he wrote so the words just flowed into the room
by themselves.

Ekelöf, Fröding and Artur Lundkvist wrote so it
sounded good read aloud. Strindberg did too, of course.
But he was different. The others were only good when
you put sound to them. But Strindberg you could read
silently too. Where old shacks stood close together . . .
and thine is the power, I have the word in my power
and other things that sounded just as good when you
read them aloud as when you saw the letters on the
spine silently. They speak either way.

Salvador Dali was like Ekelöf and Fröding and
Lundkvist, he could paint so you could hear him chewing the letters between his teeth so you saw it. He painted such funny figures in his pavilion at the World's Fair
too. It was the dream about Venus on the bottom of the
ocean with large breasts and a sofa like Greta Garbo's

lips you could sit on if you wanted. But I had only seen
the outside of the house in the amusement area beside
Admiral Byrd's Penguinland on the Loop just before you
got to Congress of Beauty where naked girls walked
around on the lawn sometimes. I pretended I wasn't
looking at them, but just walked and strolled to get to
the lake. They weren't completely naked, of course. That
wouldn't have been allowed. The police would have
come. They had little pants on. I didn't go into Dali's
exhibition either. They said you could see a kind of
aquarium there with naked girls swimming around.

I didn't really want to think about that as I walked
back and forth across the kitchen floor and declaimed
for Karna so the windowpanes shook:

> The Lord steps across Korasan
> The Lord, Lord, the last and first
> fervently he goes forth on his fury's path,
> mightily he wanders in the desert,
> his lightning flashes in the haze,
> everything his eye sees perishes,
> he who is hungry, hungers even more,
> he who is thirsty, thirsts!

I looked at Karna and opened the vowels so Ä and
Ö and Å were distinct and clear and I let my voice rise
and fill the whole kitchen around her.

A load of corn about hip-wide rocked
along the field roads
reached up to the birches and hung them
with its yellow corn hair.
The planks thundered under the load,
and in the dusk the pigs howled from hunger
and the train signalled shrill
away at the station idyll Hyllstofta—

And there were several other famous classics I liked
too and had in books. Ones that painted and drew more
like Strindberg wrote. Not as elegant as Fröding and
Lundkvist, but good. I liked Goya with war and
proverbs. And Bruegel, both paintings with people in a
landscape—especially the one with hunters in the winter
coming in from the left with the landscape under them
and the other winter scenes—and pictures he made in
Bosch's style with devils and strange houses which
turned when you looked carefully and marvelous figures
that just multiplied the more you looked. My favorite
was his engraving of the deadly sin, sloth. I could lie and
look at that and think for hours. I had seen Bruegel for
real too when I went with the class to the Metropolitan
Museum of Art. But only the harvest picture. And it
wasn't nearly as much fun as the engraving. The figures
were smaller and more formal in the painting. You
couldn't step into the painting. Bruegel had his drinking
man reach his scythe all the way out to the viewer, and
then a foot sticks out across the frame so we who were
looking at it both looked at the picture and were drawn

into it. This was something I thought about a lot. You couldn't do that with photography. Be both inside and outside.

In the same room with the Bruegel painting at the Metropolitan Museum of Art there was another picture, a little one with glass over it right by the door. You had to use a magnifying glass to look at it. A swarming Hell with little tiny devils and richly detailed burning people who were falling down from a mountain. But it was not by Bruegel and not by Bosch either or anyone else for that matter. But I used to go there to look at it.

I liked Holbein too, of course, who drew death taking one after the other. The three books about Goya, Bruegel and Holbein I had taken away from them after Christmas last year and they had never noticed. They had been given the books as presents and then forgotten them. The Holbein book was very small and fit into a pocket. The others were large oblong ones. They were in the metal suitcase which held my big shipment of books. They didn't know that. They really didn't like looking at pictures, they didn't care about *Life* and they only liked the painters they had met and could talk about at their parties. Like Tombrock, he was German or Dutch or something like that and made pictures of sad people with large faces. They had had him in the family room in Bromma and in the dining room in New York too. Like the Grünewald here.

The Aalto chairs could have been theirs. They had bought several of those Aalto chairs at Swedish Pewter before the trip. But the chairs had been stored at Frey's

Express with everything else since we moved away from
Sweden a few years ago. Aalto was famous for his chairs.
Chairs like that had been in his pavilion at the World's
Fair at home in America. Finland was the *land of forests,*
so it was obvious that Aalto and his wife, who made
their pavilion a *symphony of wood,* as they called it,
thought that bentwood chairs belong to the *world of
tomorrow.* But I didn't like them. They tilted so coldly. I
would never have chairs like that when I was able to
furnish my own place. I wouldn't have Tombrock either.
But Olson, who painted the picture with the shadow that
hung outside my door, I could take Olson.

The minutes went by slavishly slow. Time didn't
move, it just trembled. I had probably come way too
early. I said that to Aunt Elsa.

"They're not up yet, are they?" I said.

But Aunt Elsa was in a rush herself and had asked
me to hurry up so she could see I left on time.

"If I go to school and leave you alone you might get
involved in a book," she said.

I had to get tickets from them. Maybe they were out
for a walk since the weather was no nice. I wasn't
allowed to make them wait. But of course I had been
right. I had arrived too early.

Down there outside the window were Munkbron
and Riddarhustorget, all deserted in the summer morning
sun. The only thing moving was a little cloud above the
spire of St. Clara's Church. The air was completely still.
Not one ripple on the water in the canal.

Two soldiers came from Riddarholm. They strolled

across the bridge in baggy uniforms. They were middle-aged. It showed in their walk. Yes, Dunkirk was falling after Leopold's treason. The Germans bombed the ones who were trapped there. Yesterday the Germans took Adinekerke west of Furnes and Ghylevelde a mile east of Dunkirk. They took more than 200 cannons too. I had heard it on the news. The Germans had also been able to communicate that the chief of the English expeditionary corps, Lord Gort, had already fled and found safety in England and left his troops in the lurch. Generals always flee first. That's why they live so long and can win so many medals too. The Germans continued to bomb. But France would retaliate soon and chase the Germans back to their dark forests. *Weygand may have been born in Brussels, but he is not a traitor like Leopold.* The Huns would find that out.

The cloud up above stood completely summer-still over the field. Between the two black-burned leafless sprawling trees to my left was a dead horse. The stomach was bloated from gasses and the four legs sprawled. But the wind wasn't coming from that direction and the stench wasn't noticeable. I heard the sound of a motor while the group was still far away. Two motorcycles with sidecars behind an open Mercedes with standards. The general was fleeing from the French. That was the general I was waiting for. The one who carried all the secret documents from Hitler's headquarters. I took a quick look at the handwritten coded message in our private code which the messenger had brought me from General Weygand that morning. Now I lay in ambush, according

to orders. I squatted in the ditch with fieldglasses in front
of my eyes and watched the vehicles approach. They
moved forward slowly over the straight road across the
rolling plain. But I could see how they grew toward me
as the sound of the motor increased in volume. Now
they were so close I could see that the general was
wearing a monocle and had a knight's cross with oak
leaves in a black-white-red band around his neck. I put
down the fieldglasses and got ready. Now the group was
very close and the din almost deafening. With my teeth, I
pulled out the safety. I threw myself back down into the
ditch as I threw the hand grenade and the German staff
car jolted. It looked as if a red broom was erupting from
the street around the car. The driver was killed on the
spot. The general fell out of the car and blood ran in two
streams across the pavement from the broken skull. The
uniform cap with the swastika rolled away, was caught
by the wind and disappeared in the distance. Soldiers in
his body guard hopped on their motorcycles. They hurried, howling in that awful German language, weeping
and sniffling the clumsy Huns rushed toward the slaugh-
tered general and I bent smiling over the machine gun.
Then I laughed out loud in time with their howling. The
Germans were just mowed down. Some floundered as
they died. Others touched their throats. One called to
God.

"Ach, Gott, mein Gott," he screamed. Then he was
dead too.

Nothing helped against my machine gun's persistent
hammering. They were all dead. When the last one had

fallen and I had put an extra shot into each ass to assure myself that no one was just *feigning death* so he could underhandedly, as only a real Hun can do, throw himself over me with a dagger, I exhaled and wiped oil-soaked hands on my uniform pants.

Now everything was quiet. You could hear the birds singing again and high above me against the bright blue sky swallows swooped through the fresh air. The two motorcycles burned. The smoke climbed from them toward the sky. The plain was completely deserted as far as the eye could see. I got up out of the ditch and walked slowly to the dead Germans. I kicked the corpses of two German soldiers out of my way. They tumbled to the side and then over onto their stomachs like big rag dolls. I lifted up the general's remaining half-head with the tip of my toe and said:

"Well, one more Hun in Hell."

I bent down, took out my clippers and snipped off the chain that bound the black document portfolio with gold imperial eagles on it to the general's right hand and stuffed the document portfolio with all of Hitler's secret plans under my arm. The knight's cross lay on the pavement. It had been torn off in the explosion. I picked it up absent-mindedly and looked at it. Baff! I turned it over in my hand and it glittered in the sun. But you could keep it as a memento of this assignment, I thought, and stuffed it into my breast pocket. Then I trampled his monocle to pieces with my heel and walked away. The gravel crackled under my soles, the houses ahead in the village were marked by gunshots and deserted. Only a few cackling hens ran across the road and a lone black rooster stood on the dung heap and crowed. Darkening walls, straw hanging out from the openings in the haylofts, and a sweet stifling odor from the corpses which had gone unburied since the Germans passed through here during their offensive and far ahead I saw the French bombers come flying. A new stage of the war had begun and the liberator of Flanders wiped sweat from his brow, looked out squinting across the plain, held the important portfolio tight and wandered on toward his destination.

In reality the Germans just continued forward. Unless Weygand had sent in the reserves already this morning and the war turned, although it wasn't in the newspapers yet here in Sweden. I took another fistful of peanuts from the big glass bowl on the glass table. As the peanuts began to run out, figures appeared clearly in the glass. On the bottom of the bowl and up above the walls three naked girls danced and skipped around with bunches of grapes between and around them. They held up the bunches of grapes in their hands, toward the edge of the bowl, and it was as if there were bunches of grapes everywhere around them. As if they were trampling wine. You could see one girl from the front if you brushed the nuts out of the way, she was completely naked, but held her right leg as she skipped so you couldn't see her down there and two waved veils. Almost naked. They had breasts and everything and there was more to look at than Grünewald's dancing colored figure eights. I took more peanuts and traced the girls' veils in the glass with my fingertip. Their breasts stuck out. There were certainly no peanuts in Sweden. Leopold was a *traitor* and the English just fled. But the French wouldn't let the Huns conquer beautiful France.

I could hear them talking in there. I heard voices but couldn't distinguish the words. It sounded as if Alva were reading something aloud while she explained it. Now and then I heard Gunnar grunt in agreement. I could have listened to them, put my ear to the keyhole as they do in novels, but I didn't bother to do that. The envelope on the telephone table contained press clippings, I saw. It was stuffed full and half open. It lay diagonally across the table with the upper left corner a little bit under the telephone. I went to the table, pulled out the envelope and lifted the flap. On top was a clipping from *Dagens Nyheter.* It was stamped May 29, 1940. The name of the month was printed in large capital letters. Alva looked out from the two-column picture in her half profile. In her briefcase she had two new books she had written, it said in the caption.

——Now I will send the children to the country and finish writing a book on women's work during wartime, says Mrs. Myrdal, who has stepped off the train after her long and secret trip across the Atlantic, looking just as fresh as if she had only come from Göteborg.

After that the article talked about women and women's work during the last war and in this war and the success of working women in America. I didn't bother to read it. I didn't read the other clippings either. They were all the same. I knew what she usually said when she spoke with reporters about the roles of working women and slid the clippings into a pile again after I had glanced through them. I was careful to replace the envelope exactly as it had been before I opened it. No one could see I had read it.

It was a summer morning. A real Swedish early summer morning with bright water and blue sky and clear air and green foliage around the stately Riddarhuset, the House of Nobility, which is such a fine memorial to the history of our country, I would have said to reporters if I had been that way and I sat in the window seat and waited and looked out across Monkbron toward Riddarhustorget because I had come entirely too early, exactly as I had thought, but no one listened to me.

"Now when I walked across the Flemish plain..." I began to think almost out loud, but then I didn't feel like continuing the story any more.

It was as if it had no color any more. And actually it wasn't much fun with the dead Germans in the road because of the many dead there in Flanders now that the war was really on. They had died for real and smelled for real like in Petsamo outside the factory. It was difficult terrain so they had been left frozen stiff for a long time before they could dig holes and bury them after the war.

"It was like a huge woodpile."

And they lie all the way under the surface of the earth now. I went there and looked and wondered whether there was a hand sticking up somewhere. There wasn't. But there was a smell coming from the earth. Then I walked too far out among the small birches on the tundra to piss and the major called to me because there was a mine field there which had not been cleared. I found the helmet there. A Russian soldier's helmet with a red star and a hole right through the metal. The major took out the inside lining that was moldy and I thought the brain had run out through there. Or maybe it was one of those helmets on which the Finnish recruits practiced marksmanship. A man crouched way down in the ditch and held the helmet on a stick and suddenly he stuck it up a little. Then the recruits were supposed to catch sight of it all at the same time, aim and shoot. It could be a helmet like that. I had taken that along to Sweden without Alva noticing. Now it was in safe storage at Elsa and Gösta's house, in their closet.

I had been staying with them in Solna almost a week now, ever since we had arrived in Sweden. They had a four-room apartment and I had to sleep on a daybed in their den, where they had a desk and reference books and a radio. It was a large bright room with a bay window. Elsa was Gunnar's sister. She was married to Gösta, but he had been called up now and was somewhere out in the archipelago. He got to come home sometimes on leave. They were both teachers and used to boys like me and had two children of their own, so they could easily have me with them too, thought Gunnar. I had lived there before and they said I was going to live there this fall too.

I often lived with them. Even when I was small and

lived at Grandfather and Grandmother's house at Gesta, Elsa took care of me sometimes when Grandmother was busy or needed to rest. At that time, Gösta and Elsa were only engaged. He visited Elsa at Gesta and she and he took me out for long walks and to look at rock carvings. Before we went to America I had lived with them and gone to school in Sigtuna. They were elementary school teachers there, both of them. I had gone to Sigtuna Elementary School and not to Sigtuna School, because it was expensive and served only the upper class, said Alva. When the family was in Sweden we children lived with one of our grandparents or with Gunnar or Alva's siblings or with other relatives when Gunnar and Alva were away on vacation or needed time to work. We had done that as long as I could remember. Children were so disturbing in a city apartment when you were trying to read. It was better for the children in the country too. I had grown up in Gunnar's father's house. Later, when they had a house, a babysitter took care of the small children or they were sent to Alva's sister, Rut, who was married to Elon and lived in the country on a farm at Tillberga.

　　These days it was especially important that Gunnar and Alva had time for concentrated work without being disturbed. It was best for me too. It was better for me with Elsa and Gösta, who were used to boys my age, Alva said when she talked to them about it, and as far as the small children were concerned, Grandmother could take care of them because there really wasn't any space for children and babysitter in the apartment they had borrowed for the summer. There wasn't even a maid's room for a housekeeper, and Gunnar and Alva had to be content with day help while they waited for Per Albin to decide what he wanted Gunnar to do. They ate out. They had guests at home only for drinks and appetizers. But I didn't actually know how many rooms there were in the apartment because this was the first time I had been here. Now the peanuts were almost gone.

This war had been going on for almost a year now. If you wanted to, you could think of Europe as a huge sandbox, with the high Alps at the bottom and rivers and plains up here where small swarming armies moved while the generals and politicians stood around, pointed down at them with long sticks and shoved the armies around down in the sand. You could also turn it around and see Death himself come to them, one after the other. Make pictures of that. Death took generals by the arm in the middle of the barrack yard and he tapped reporters on the shoulder at the streetcar stop and he took off his hat and bowed deeply to dancing girls at the ball and at first he looked like an ordinary person, a soldier or waiter or young gentleman, but when they looked carefully to see who it was they saw the chest was open and hollow under the clothes and they saw the wide grin and then understood. It showed in their big eyes. But then it was all over and too late.

"And the moon shone on the bones of the dead and the bones reflected the moonlight!"

They were still talking inside the room. I waited for Alva and chewed on peanuts they had brought from

America. Planter's Peanuts. The suitcase with summer clothes which Aunt Elsa had packed was in the hall, but I was supposed to get a ticket and pocket money for the whole summer from Alva, they had said, and I was taking the 11:45 train from Central Station. It was the only morning train that stopped at Karlsro outside Norrköping. It was only a train stop, not a real station. But the ticket to Karlsro was 20 öre cheaper than the ticket to Norrköping.

Gunnar had opened the door when I rang the bell. He was wearing blue striped pajamas and a red dressing gown with a black belt. He had yellow leather slippers. In his hand he held *Morgontidningen*, as *Socialdemokraten* was called now that there was war.

"Well, if it isn't Jannie," he had said. "Are you coming to visit our little student digs so early in the morning?"

Then he laughed because he knew I was supposed to come today in the morning to get my ticket and said:

"It was probably Elsa who sent you on your way so early. She's always so worried about missing the train. She gets that from Mother. Mother can leave the waiting room and then stand half an hour out on the deserted platform to wait for the train."

He pushed the newspaper into the pocket of his dressing gown. He patted me on the head and said:

"The world is a dark place now. First Spain and then Poland, which is already gone, and then Finland and Denmark and Norway and Holland and Belgium and now it's France's turn. Yes, Jan, if you but knew with how little wisdom the world is governed. Now as formerly. You can put your suitcase here in the hall and sit down and wait a little while in the living room and Alva will come soon. There are some peanuts, too, left from last night. They're in a glass bowl on the table. You can take some if you like. There may be some olives left too."

Maybe they were still eating breakfast. But now that they didn't get it in bed and had to get up and make it themselves, it shouldn't take such a long time. Black coffee with toast and marmalade. Not even butter because that was fattening and in America they drank apple juice, but I didn't know if there was such a thing in Sweden. Most likely they had finished breakfast long ago and they were now going through the morning papers talking about what had happened in the world. *Posten* probably hadn't come yet. It took a long time to read all the newspapers. So it wasn't strange that Alva took a while. I told Elsa from the beginning Alva would do that. I would be too early. But she didn't think it mattered much. The main thing was not to be late. She had always hated to be late. Besides, she wanted to see that I started out properly before she herself had to go to school.

On a morning like this there was a lot to discuss. I used to do that myself at home in New York. I was the very first to wake up and I listened to my radio and heard the news and thought. Now I had listened to the radio at Elsa and Gösta's. Eden said the English had immediately rushed to assist when Belgium asked for help and had taken a position at Schelde. They had been

advancing for ten days, but then because of circumstances beyond their control they had been unable to
hold on. They had been able to retreat to Dunkirk in a
brilliant manner. I didn't think so. They had only demonstrated stupidity. They should have been able to control
the circumstances. All you had to do was look at the
map. Hitler had lured them. The attack on Belgium was
only a trick. The Maginot line was too strong to be
stormed. The idea was to lure the English and French
into a corner and then hit what was left. He did that.
And now he tied a noose around Dunkirk. Anyone who
was interested in maps could have seen he would do
that. It was only generals who were so stupid they didn't
understand anything. But they were the first to flee too.
Terboven had made a speech in Oslo and promised
Norway huge markets in southern Europe and eastern
Europe and Roosevelt wants to be supreme commander
but Vandenberg and his like *try to stop him. They are like
Leopold. They are traitors.* Shoot them! But if I said such
a thing so someone heard, Alva would just sigh and say:

"But Jannie!"

So I never said things like that out loud. I just saw
it. The senator was led away through the ice cold cellar
corridor and *the gates of death were opened unto him
and as he saw the doors of the shadow of death he shrank
in fear* and I raised my hand and gave the order and
Bang! the isolationist Vandenberg took the shot in the
neck *he so well deserved.*

But Vandenberg was smooth and would be the
Republican president if Roosevelt lost and then there

would be no one to lead America and resist Hitler.

Yes, I had seen his friends, I said. I've seen the Fritz Kuhn Association parade down First Avenue. *With the Stars and Stripes and the Nazi swastika flag up front.* * They tramped forward *row upon row.* Black pants, white shirts with swastikas and black caps, Legionnaires' caps they were. And from their delicatessens *the Krauts who had just got their citizenship papers came tumbling out waving their heinie-wursts and all shouting Heil Hitler! Heil Hitler! more Geldsendungen nach Deutschland! more Weihnachts-Lebensmittelpakete! Sieg Heil! and the Bund marches ever on until victory is ours!* called the Krauts. I had seen them there just as I had seen them in Hötorget before we moved to America. But though there were many more over there we knew how to handle them.

Down at Union Square where I used to go because there was always a lot to see and because the movie theaters were just as good but much cheaper than *the ones at Times Square* I had once actually seen them run from the police batons. It was last summer. I had been at the World's Fair, but left early and went into town. Three Bundists had come to sell their newspaper. It was called *Weckruf,* but also *The Free American.* Newspaper hawkers like that were almost never seen there around Union Square. Reds were almost always the only ones there.

I told Karna about this later in the summer. They had come with their Bundist caps and their newspapers and people didn't like that. A crowd of people gathered around them. They took the newspapers away and final-

ly they almost ran for the subway to get away. And I said
that the Bund leaders must have given them orders.
Maybe it was something those three had to do to prove
they weren't cowards. Kuhn might have *asked them if
they had a yellow streak down their backs or if they were
white men.*

   "Well, prove it!"

   "Is that so," she said.

   I had told John more. How they were beaten up.
Later in the spring I made it even worse. That time it was
for Nelson, after I had been to Chicago and seen how
the Communists were beaten up by the Legionnaires
when they were trying to sell *New Masses.* It had been
ugly and the Nazis should have been locked up instead.

   I said I had seen them as they came walking toward
the park. And they were afraid now that they had
reached Union Square. I could see it in the way they
walked with short steps close beside each other. They
didn't have complete uniforms, just the black caps. A
few people were already going after them, then more
and more. Farther on they knocked the Bundists' caps
off. The tallest of the three Bundists was almost bald. He
had only a wreath of hair around his head, even though
he didn't look particularly old. He was swarthy and
probably not more than thirty or thirty-five. The three
stood close together, completely still and quiet. Then
they took the newspapers away from the Bundists and
threw them in the garbage can. They offered no
resistance. They didn't dare. But the bald Bundist *must
have said something about niggers* because suddenly a

black man turned around and hit him right in the face with his fist. Here at Union Square it wasn't like in other neighborhoods. It wasn't like Harlem where everyone was black, but here too the blacks had their *pride*.

And now as I told Nelson about it I heard the Bundist scream and saw him bend forward. He started to spit and vomit and I think he lost a few teeth. He was very bloody in any case, and he spit blood and whimpered a little. The two other Bundists ran. Everyone laughed all around and the black man hit the Bundist one more time right in the face. But this time just with the open flat of his hand. Like a slap on the ear. There was a smack. Then the black man talked to him.

"Say after me: Please forgive me for being a Nazi swine."

At first the Bundist didn't want to say anything. He stood still, bent forward a little and blood dripped from his mouth. By now there were a lot of people standing around. They all yelled that the Bundist had to say it. They stood close, close around him and screamed at him. I worked my way through the crowd to see better what was happening. People were polite and made room for me. The Bundist was trapped like a rat in a corner, standing in the middle of the circle. He leaned against a park bench for support. The crown of his head was shining with sweat and he looked very small.

"Well," said the black man. *"We are all waiting."*

Now they had stopped laughing and yelling and it got quiet. Only the traffic was heard and then the bald guy began to cry. It was a swarthy bald guy who stood cowering and when he *began to talk* we heard he spoke poor English. A real sinister Kraut.

"Please forgive me for being a Nazi swine," said the Bundist quietly.

"Louder," said the black man. *"We want to hear you say it loud and clear."*

"Please forgive me for being a Nazi swine," screamed the Bundist loudly.

"Well, folks," said the black man, smiling. *"Do we forgive him?"*

They all laughed again and now the traffic couldn't be heard any more because they laughed so much and began to step to the side. There was an opening in the crowd now. Like a corridor. The Bundist began to run. He stumbled and fell, but landed on his open hands and stopped a brief moment like an animal on all fours with his head hanging. Everyone looked at him but no one stepped forward to even touch him. Then he got up again and ran to the subway.

Nelson wasn't sure I had been there, I saw that in his face, but he didn't contradict me because we both believed that was what you should do with Bundists and I quickly changed the subject so he wouldn't be able to ask questions.

But here in this country no one was allowed to say anything against the Nazis. Big signs had been set up saying "Quiet" and "Public Responsibility" and "Troubled Times." When Hitler sent his Germans here members of the government would stand in front and bow. Just like in Denmark. But you weren't allowed to say that either.

The sky was still pure clear blue, although early morning was turning into late morning. Even the clouds were gone. They had almost unnoticeably slowly drifted away above the city toward the country while I was telling my story. Then I remembered. For a moment it was almost hard to breathe.

Last night I had been awakened by a dream when it was only very early morning and everyone was sleeping and the park in front of Elsa and Gösta's was very quiet and I had got up and stood a long time in the bay window and looked out the window and just watched although the dream was clear in my mind the whole time. I didn't know whether I wanted to think about this dream, but it was a dream I remembered. Not everything that happened in the dream, of course, but the very end. They had gone down the steps and we had seen them go and I don't know exactly who they were but the staircase had worn-down marble treads and we saw them from above and behind and one of them, the man to the right, had a black overcoat. We were watching, I and a girl. The girl was a little like Eloise, my second cousin in Willmar, or like Barbara in school, the one with the bangs I had told Karna so much about. We stood at the window later and I think it was my room on Kungsholmstrand a long time ago or maybe in New York. It was night and there were stars and I felt almost ready to weep and the girl was Stella and pointed. Then I saw she had diagonal scratches up her thigh and across her stomach although I didn't think she was naked and she said:

"They're scratching. You can hear it."

I saw that she was a completely naked girl, a completely naked Eloise or a naked Barbara right in front with her head turned away and I reached out my hand and touched her and woke up suddenly and even if the dream hadn't been as well thought out as a fantasy and not even as clear as one of my fantasies, it was much stronger. No fantasy feels like that.

I stared down across Munkbron and it took several minutes for the dream feeling to go away. The scratches had been very clear. The peanuts were gone. The bowl was totally empty. I didn't want to turn around and look down into it and see the girls dancing even though I should have wanted to do that. The door would open any time now and Alva would come out and see me.

I didn't see any cars. No traffic at all. Not even pedestrians. The soldiers were gone. A long time ago they had disappeared from in front of the Riddarhuset, the House of Nobles. Empty as a theater stage after the company has left. *Empty and silent.* And that is why the air is so clear. It is empty here. *A small town to the north in Europe.* The letters took shape as a title diagonally across the green roof of Riddarhuset.

That is a beginning. A statement. A quiet picture and letters which come one after the other heavy and black. Now, with Ciné-Kodak Kodachrome and letters in complementary colors. Brilliant red letters diagonally across the green roof. There is a lot of green and blue in Sweden in the summertime. It would work on color film. But I wasn't sure whether north in this context should be

"north" or "North," so I put the whole title in capital letters *A SMALL TOWN FAR TO THE NORTH IN EUROPE*.
The letters barely had room. I saw that. I could look for
really nice letters that were a little smaller, of course, and
cut them out and paste into the color pictures one after
the other so I could do the whole thing with the help of
Kodak-Titles. But that wouldn't be neater. Better to take
three color pictures of the motif. Begin with a sweeping
view of Stockholm. Then come in closer with each picture. First title: *IN EUROPE*. Second title: *FAR TO THE
NORTH*. Third title: *A SMALL TOWN*. I would lay it precisely on the roof with the cloud above and it would be
neat.

But I wouldn't be up here long enough to make the
film. The New York film I had been working on since
February never was completed either. In that one I didn't
begin with written text. It was much more stylish to *title
by implication*. I worked with automatic shutter triggers
and the film began with a full-length picture of me while
I sat in the chair reading, then a close-up so you saw I
was reading *Gateway to Adventure* and I held the book
so the title was clearly visible for several seconds. After
that I added a night picture of Broadway and a close-up
of the sign for a liquor store with an old man holding up
a bottle and in a speech bubble it said "*THAT'S GOOD
WHISKEY.*" That's how the film began. It portrayed life in
New York. And I had thought out the ending carefully.
People like small ants against the Trylon and the
Perisphere at the World of Tomorrow. But I had only
been able to afford to buy a few rolls of panchromatic

film before leaving. So it was never completed although I had thought out almost the whole film in detail to get real *continuity* so one thing led into the other first along Broadway and from night to workday to evening and the lighted exhibition.

Continuity when you tell a story on film means you don't have to use stupid captions. *Continuity* is just as important as holding the camera still. Otherwise it is just various *shots*. Alva and Gunnar didn't understand that. They asked people to pose and then photographed them with the movie camera rather than letting something happen in the picture. They jerked and swung the camera and didn't dare let the film roll, but wanted to save film by shooting short, short sequences of pictures and then they didn't understand how to edit. Gunnar had stopped taking movies after a mishap with the first roll, but Alva kept on even though she didn't really understand anything when I explained to her how it should be done. It was I who picked out the camera for them too. That was why they didn't get just a fixed focus camera, but the best model, Ciné-Kodak Eight, Model 60 with F.1.9 lens which would work in near darkness. And that was in spite of their instructions to get only the simplest and cheapest 8-millimeter camera. Because they didn't know anything I could do what was best. Alva had said no, though, when I thought they should also have a one-and-a-half inch telephoto lens with F.4.5.

They didn't understand what film was even though they went to movies sometimes. Little had been said about things like continuity and when to use close-ups and how to edit one scene to the next in drama class in school, but I had read a lot myself in the school library before I got them to buy the camera. In school, we had frequently discussed the question of how to begin a spoken or written story. Not only in my class. The teachers had also gathered all the students and let four writers of detective novels discuss how to begin a story. They sat up on the stage and the one who wrote about Nero Wolfe said that you should never forget the audience.

"Now the butler opens the door and the man of the house is lying dead in front of the open fireplace. If you write that in the first line of the first page the reader will yawn and put the book aside. You know who it is on the floor dead and you have thought a long time about him, but the reader knows nothing. You have to get the reader interested right from the beginning. That's the trick. You can begin in a street instead. Or with a description of a scene. Or write that you are the one standing and looking at a house and you know there is a dead body inside. That gets their interest. But you always have to have a beginning."

It was a little different with film. There you could just as well begin with the butler opening the door and the body lying there, I thought. That was an image. And a picture of a body was a good opening if it was going to be a detective film. But this was a different kind of film.

So a statement would make a good beginning. Or maybe do something completely different. Begin with the cloud going past. Then Riddarhuset and then jump from there to the sandstone woman here above the entrance and then take other figures and finally the whole door and sidewalk. If the sun was right later in the afternoon the facade might look wonderful in Kodachrome, which makes deep red look so good. You could put the titles there. But they had already told me that in Sweden where film was so expensive it was out of the question that I would be allowed to play any more with the good movie camera. That was that.

And they wouldn't have liked the film. A PALACE FOR PETTERSSON, it could be called. Here in the window seat high up in the Petersén house I sat next to a big round cactus and waited. Grandfather would have laughed if he had heard that Gunnar was residing in the Petersen Palace. A real palace for one who was born Pettersson, then took the name Myrdal to ennoble the family.

I had laughed myself when Gösta told me they had rented there. It was near everything, Alva had said to Elsa on the phone. I knew which house it was. I had been on a school field trip here when I took local history and read about Stockholm at the Swedish elementary school in Älsten. We had stood on Munkbron and Miss Rehn had clapped her hands and pointed and said:

"Listen now! Look over here. This is how they built in Queen Christina's time! This is the best example Stockholm has of a rich man's house from the 1600s. On this property Göran Persson had a house with a cabbage patch. The palace itself was built between the years 1645 and 1647 by a master builder from Leipzig in Germany

who was called Döteber. It was built for Reinhold
Leuhusen who was later given a noble title and became
lieutenant governor of Stockholm. The family had come
from the Netherlands two hundred years earlier and was
very significant here in our city. Anna Reinholdsdotter
Leuhusen was, for example, abbess at the Convent of St.
Claire when Gustavus Adolphus rode into Stockholm. It
is called the Petersen house because it was owned later
by a wholesaler Pettersson of the East India Company
who married into a rich family and was given the title 'af
Petersen.' This house is the finest example we have of
the German-Dutch Renaissance. Look carefully at the
double portals."

The next day we had to draw and then color the
whole facade in our Write-Draw notebooks and write all
the names and years beside. So I knew very well where
Gunnar had rented. One who was descended from
Petterssons in a Petersen palace but the title 'af Petersen'
we didn't get. Alva did become mysterious sometimes
and thought she actually was some sort of Celsing from a
side branch of the family. Maybe an elegant girl who had
fallen in love with a farmhand. But I had asked Folke
about it and he had said that it was something only Alva
and Lova, their mother, believed. Not even a student was
to be found among their ancestors. Most of them were
small farmers and farmhands. Only a few of them had
been a little better off. Folke had in fact researched what
they chit-chatted about with that business of Celsings,
but the only thing he found was that my great-great-
great-great-grandfather's name was not found in any

church registers and my great-great-great-grandfather had been known for being well dressed. So much for the nobility!

And now a blue streetcar swung down toward Munkbron from the stop at Riddarhustorget. I couldn't see the number yet. I screwed up my eyes. In spite of my glasses I couldn't get a clear look at the number sign. And how the streetcar lines in the little city of Stockholm twisted and circled I had *plain forgotten.*

I had come on the number three. Had stood at the back of the front car with my suitcase. Only the one and three and nine came out here. It was a number one passing by now below. I never took the nine. On the four you could ride all around the city. The seven went to Djurgården. But that was so long ago. I lived in Sweden then, took the twelve and went to Ålsten elementary school. Now I had come on the fifteen from Elsa and Gösta's and changed at Norra Bantorget which was the end of the line.

Now I was going down to relatives near Norrköping. Grandmother had called Elsa about it. She had also asked Alva to get a ticket. That was the least she could do! I was going to live with Robert and Greta until it was time to begin school. Robert was Gunnar's little brother and had become head of Marieborg Folk High School outside Norrköping. There was lots of room, especially now when there was no course in progress. Grandmother was there and visited over the summer. And all my cousins in that branch of the family. Aunt Elsa would come down too as soon as school was out. She would tutor me so I would be ready to get back into a Swedish school.

I must remember to tell the conductor properly that I am to get off at Karlsro. Aunt Elsa had said that several times before she gave me the packed sandwiches. Karlsro was just a place where the train didn't stop if there was no one getting on and no passengers had said they wanted to get off. I was just waiting now for them to get ready to send me on my way. As soon as Alva opened the door and gave me the ticket and envelope with pocket money for the summer, I could take my suitcase from the hall and go. But no door opened and the sky outside had already started to get its late morning color above Riddarhuset.

Time goes so slowly when you are waiting, I said. We sat smoking in our dug-out. No one in the platoon answered. This was our third day of readiness. The only things we had to eat were old rusks. We soaked them in water and chewed thoughtfully. We couldn't get bread up here at the front line any more. But we made coffee in the cooling mantles of the gun turrets. But you could taste oil in the coffee then. It had started to rain too. Time went slowly.

Then it started. We heard whistles in the air above us and the ground shook from the dull thunder in front. Now this year's spring offensive had begun. It was our artillery starting to shoot into the German lines. Nelson lifted the telephone receiver. Then he put it aside.

"The line is dead," he said.

"All we can do is wait," I said.

Three hours later, from our *shell-hole* between *the stumps of trees,* I could see a cloud up high above. It drifted away over what remained of the Red House. The house we have fought over for three springs already. We had left the front line. Now we were way out in no-man's-land. We had crawled out from under the barbed wire when *the runner came with our orders* and lay waiting now in the clay hole and crouched. Now and then the clay rose like a great broom coming up from the ground and it rained mud and gravel on us when their grenades hit.

"*Some forest that,*" said Nelson and waved his thumb at the shot-up stubble in what had once been an oak forest. A grenade hit the ground close by.

I saw that Nelson's cheek had been cut open by shrapnel, but it was nothing to worry about he thought and the first aid station was a long way behind us anyway.

"*Just a small scratch,*" he says. But I see it's bleeding a lot. His tunic is full of blood and his face is white from pain and I can see all the way to his jawbone. He won't make it through the day. But he was a *good guy.* We will remember him, we survivors, as we sit in the shithouse and smoke and talk about comrades who have already moved on. But Nelson acts like he's going to live.

Then the sergeant comes creeping up. He bellows something. But what he says cannot be heard in the increasing cannon thunder which seems to be rising to a crescendo. He waves and we get up reluctantly and run crouching so we won't get hit by bullets whizzing past. We throw ourselves down again and notice that the Germans have started to push their way toward us with the grenade thrower. I hear the dull sound of explosions very nearby. Gravel and sand spray over me. I take out a spade and dig a trench. Something rolls over the edge like a muddy potato sack. It is the sergeant. He is already dead. I get blood on my hands when I take out his wallet.

"He was OK," whispers Nelson, who is already a *goner.*

"Yes," I say. "I'll send his last letter back to the wife in Willmar."

Nelson is too weak to answer now and I think about what I'll write to his parents. I have to think of something. Only we old combat soldiers can understand this. I'll have to beautify all this. They don't need to know how he suffered. Like the horse with its stomach cut open lying between the lines with flies crawling in its guts and screaming with open mouth. No, I'll write that it went quickly.

If we stand still the Germans will put an end to us. Their grenades hit the ground close by. If we try to get back to our own lines again we will be shot as deserters as they had already shot Jones and Smith and Theobald and Rosenthal and Mr. Francis. Staff officers will rise from their lunch tables. Drain their glasses. Belch a little. Condemn us to death for cowardice. Have us shot behind the storage shed.

I get up on my knees in the muddy soup while the

grenades howl past me and wave my arms above my head.

"I'm taking command," I cry. "Forward!"

When we go *over the top* I see that Nelson is still lying there. He's on his back in the mud with arms stretched out and mouth gaping.

"He was the last to go," I say. *"The last but one."*

Then he disappears in a huge explosion and alone I lead my men toward the German lines. I have taken my trench-knife between my teeth and get ready for whatever is going to happen.

I continued to wait and they were still talking in there and I wondered if they had forgotten that I was sitting here. I was supposed to go to Central Station and take the quarter-to-twelve train south and Elsa had said I should be down there in plenty of time because there were so many people on the train now during the war. There were big delays too. I had to make sure I got on and got a seat. If they took much longer I would maybe have to stay.

CHAPTER 4

The train south stands still in Sweden and it is warm. Up front the locomotive hisses slowly. It is stuffy from the crowd of people in the car and coal dust in the nose and old men talk behind me. It is now almost 2:30 in the afternoon Monday, June 3, 1940, and it has already been more than two-and-a-half hours since we left Stockholm's Central Station. We are still standing on the track waiting just beyond Södertälje South. It is the second time we have stood like this on a side track with the steam going. A local train went north half an hour ago. A slow-moving military transport has just passed us, also going south. I know it is not a regular freight train because I saw cannons on the flatcars. Five of these in a row with guards' cars in front and behind. The outlines of the cannons were visible under the green tarpaulins.

I watched the train move away and you could begin a film like that. In toward a face in the foreground right after the title. Unshaven. Takes cigarette from lips and says:

"We shared everything. Even the lice."

Then you see that the speaker is sitting on a flatcar in the shelter of cannons and the train moves away into the landscape.

I had seen many films about the last Great War. At least once a week I had gone to Ninety-second Street where the movie theater was. It was called Nemo. There used to be war films and the kinds of films where they danced. In America you could come and go as you wished, in the middle of the film if you wanted, and you could stay in the theater as long as you wanted to. I used to sit almost all the way in the front on the left and watch films several times.

Grand Illusion I had seen not only twice on the same bill with Shirley Temple in between, but I had gone back and seen it two more times even though I couldn't stand Shirley Temple and mostly closed my eyes when she was on the screen. In the film they all spoke their own languages, German and English and French and Russian. And Erich von Stroheim played the flyer who was badly burned and got to be kommandant of the prison. His name was Rauffenstein and he said whatever happened, time was running out for aristocrats like himself and the French nobility. And the Jew Rosenthal and mechanic Maréchal help each other escape. The war is a grand illusion, but we have to win, says Maréchal and then it ends with them reaching Switzerland and they start up the snowy slope.

But our train is still standing still waiting. I sit crowded in with military men closest to me in the window seat and have my back to the whole jam-packed car because I was first when the train came in. I almost always am. If I wanted, I could look out on the landscape on the other side of the windowpane, but I sit completely still and somewhere far away the night dream is still there and now that I have made myself alone I can think about it. The one with the scratches who had been Stella was not Eloise. As I thought about it, her name was a dream feeling, gone, and now it was last winter. Eloise had *cherub knees*. She said that. She was the only one who had them. I stand in the open door and look into the room. They slept in the same bed, all five sisters. The eldest on the far right and the youngest on the left. Each had her own pink pillow with white lace and a single thin blanket with one of those flowery American quilt covers. The bed was very large and the room had fluffy white curtains. There is a rag rug on the floor and there is no threshold in the doorway where I am standing. They don't have any thresholds in the house, they usually don't have them out here. To my left inside the room is the half open door. The glossy white door-panel shines. The picture stands completely still.

It almost looks like a picture in one of the old American storybooks, left open on the table in the school library after the little children had been there for story hour one day in February. It was before anything had been said about summer and even before we were going to move to Brooklyn in the fall and long before the MS *Mathilda Thordén*. I had come to the school library to read one more time in *Popular Science* from 1917 about early experiments with hang gliders and how you can build such a hang glider yourself. During that war when Germans were always called Huns no one wanted to give any credit to Otto Lilienthal, who developed the hang glider and the basic knowledge that the

Wright brothers used, because he was German. But there was a description of how a hang glider could be built. And if we went to the same place on Long Island again I would be able to get up speed on the steep slope leading down to the bay and then *glide out over the sea to Huntington or further,* I had thought. When I came in I went to the open book and discovered that the sisters were there in the picture, lying in a row and in the book someone was standing in the doorway looking at them exactly as I had seen them for real here in Willmar. But in the picture in the book there was no rag rug on the floor. There was sunshine outside the window too and no winter darkness like here.

This is how it was done in the Old Country, they thought.. Mabel, who was eldest, had said that it was a Swedish custom for all the sisters in the family to sleep in the same bed. I didn't believe it. I had never heard of that except in stories about trolls. The only real people I remembered who slept in the same bed with the rest of the family were Njal and Bergtora with Tord, their grandson, between them. But that was when they knew attackers were coming to burn their house down on top of them. The bailiff spread a sheep skin over them and Tord lay down, he too, even though he was but a child, for people should remember him. Miss Rehn had read to us about that during library hour in Ålsten Elementary School. This was an ancient story, not everyday custom. Never had Grandmother or anyone else who used to tell about how hard things had been in the old days and in Dalecarlia talked about five sisters sleeping in the same bed. But Mabel was still very Swedish. She had been born here in Minnesota, but could not speak a single word of English when she started school, she said. They were all Swedes around here. But now it was different. They were Americans now and there weren't many who spoke Swedish any more except those who belonged to the Lutheran church.

"Grandfather Albert was a Baptist already when he immigrated," she said.

This was one evening in Willmar last Christmas and suddenly Eloise is standing in the doorway again instead of Mabel. She's wearing a blue *turtleneck sweater* with short white sleeves she had knit herself and a gray pleated skirt and now she's swinging her skirt and saying:

"See! I have cherub knees too!"

We are cousins and she is one year older than I. She was born in 1926 and will be fourteen in the spring. It was her grandfather, my great uncle Albert, who had left Gustafs fifty years before, in 1888, and taken the train to Gothenburg to emigrate to America. Grandfather had gone with him to the Solvarbo train stop to say goodbye when his older brother, Albert, departed. Grandfather was thirteen years old then and had just begun working in the forest. Grandmother told me about this when I lived with her in the house in Mariefred after Grandfather had died and Gesta was sold. She read to me too from Albert's letters home to the relatives in Sweden. That was how I already knew who was who when I met them.

It was not just one brother who left, but two. Albert

and Johan. Johan had not succeeded in America. Things had gone badly for him and he had died a long time ago and no one wanted to talk about him. Unpleasant things are not discussed. Especially not among relatives. It took several years for me to find out Grandfather had two brothers who had gone to America. Not until we got to New York did Gunnar tell me Grandfather had accompanied two brothers to the train stop and that one had succeeded in America and prospered in Minnesota, where he had had a long life and was still living, while the other had failed. He had gone to Texas where he amounted to nothing and then he died young on the East Coast, possibly while trying to get back to Solvarbo. I still don't know exactly what went wrong for him or even if he was married or if he had children or if I have cousins in that branch of the family too. And I don't know how he died. Only that he died and that it was in New York during the Great War. But I had thought sometimes about this great uncle Johan as I walked the streets of Lower Manhattan. Maybe he had walked here with no idea what to do, I thought. And I particularly thought of him when the Swedish bookkeeper came to our apartment on Riverside Drive just before Christmas last winter when I was packing for the trip west. He wanted help getting home to Sweden. He had an uncertain smile and his body cringed a little when he shook hands. After he said his American name he added:

"John, that's Johan, because I actually come from Sundbyberg."

"He doesn't go outdoors much," said Gunnar after

he had gone. "You can see it on him."

He had hung himself later that evening, it said in the *New York Times*. He hung himself in Central Park right before Christmas, two days before I went to Chicago on the way to Minnesota.

"He was weak," Gunnar said on the way to the station. "No one can help a person who can't get a grip on himself."

Things had gone well for great-uncle Albert in any case. As they had for Grandfather. But he had not become sick and died. He was old now but still lived in St. Paul and his eldest son, Gunnar's cousin, had become director of a bank out here in Willmar a hundred miles directly west as the crow flies. He had six children. Five daughters and a son. The son was called John and was one year younger than I. Eloise was second youngest of the sisters. I look at her and don't know whether the special thing about her is her laugh or the way she walks or her eyes or something else. But she is the sister everyone thinks is pretty. But she was not only pretty, she was a gal—not only a lass, but something more, something different. Her eyes screw up and are gray. I feel it when she is nearby. Now when I hear her voice I look up and see her and her newly knit sweater fits snugly. I heard her mother tell her this, but Eloise just laughed. And now as I look at her I can see clearly that it's true; the turtleneck sweater is tight. I can see that it stretches so you can see she has breasts and I swallow.

Actually I was sitting at a desk in John's den and getting ready to blow water on a model to make the

Japanese paper stretch over the new balsa wood wing when she was suddenly standing in the doorway talking to me. I had my mouth full of water and knew I looked stupid with blown-up cheeks. John was there too somewhere in the room behind me. It was him I was visiting. They had sent me west to the American relatives in Minnesota that Christmas. Maybe they were going to have parties or go on trips. Or maybe they wanted some peace away from the children, as Gunnar used to say. I don't know what they did with my sisters. Found accommodations for them somewhere, probably, because there was no one at home except the Irishwoman to take care of them. Ingrid had gone home to Sweden when the war started and Karna had gone with her because she was sick.

"*See,*" said Eloise now and stood in the doorway to John's den and swung the gray skirt and behind her the sisters were laughing. "*I have cherub knees too!*"

She did. She was standing still now and held the skirt up above her knees. Above the white knee socks you could see real small faces on her kneecaps. It was exactly like in the newspaper, she said. Cherubs. She had looked at them in the mirror and they probably brought good luck, the sisters said. But I sat there with my mouth full of water and looked at Eloise's knees with small faces bulging on them and knew deep inside me without looking up that her sweater was tight. I wanted to look as though I had barely heard what she said and was actually thinking about something else and didn't even really look because I didn't want her to see I was looking at her when I later had to say something in response and had to blow out the water so it made a silly snort and then lift my face to look into her gray eyes. She was the cutest and she knew it, that's why she was wearing that sweater, and I was afraid she noticed I often looked at her secretly when no one was watching me. I looked at her this way only because she was cute, as they said. There were a lot of girls here in America who made themselves cute. It was different with her. She was not only cute but a different kind of girl. The way she stood, maybe. Or the warm tones of her skin. She was actually not at all sweet in the same way as American girls with bows in their hair, cold white skin, red cheeks and lots of teeth.

Eloise stood with her legs a little bit apart and held up the gray skirt and I suddenly had to look away too quickly and straight at the airplane wing I was holding when I heard Olle's voice speaking Swedish:

"Just turn the girl upside down and stick your hands under the skirt right into her bush and then put your fingers under her nose afterward so she can see she smells like fish between the legs!"

It was not as if anyone could hear and Eloise didn't understand Swedish anyway, but no one was allowed to see I had heard and I thought:

"Turn Eloise with the scratched legs upside down!"

And in America they didn't say it like that.

"ALBWT, all love begins with a toss," the girls had

---

*The Girl Scouts were from the KFUK and the boys chanted Kitla Fittan Under Kjolen (Tickle the cunt under the skirt).

yelled when we threw snowballs at them in Ålsten.

"Ha, ha, ha! Love begins with a toss!" they yelled and sneered at us and jumped up and down.

"No, throwing makes you horny," we had said after we had caught them and rubbed snow in their faces.

And when there was war with Ängby and we sat watch up in the tree we had shouted at the Girl Scouts on an excursion to Judah Forest as they walked past down below on the path:

"TCUS! Tickle the cunt under the skirt! TCUS!"*

And their leader shook her fist at us and said she might have to talk to our parents but we from Olovslund were out on reconnaissance on the other side of Drottingholmsvägen where no one knew us and she didn't know who we were so we just laughed at her and her anger as we sat up in the pine and we went on yelling at the Girl Scouts that they should grab their cunts and then they went away faster than fast as we shouted after them.

"Cunts, cunts!"

That was how we had talked in Olovslund and we talked like that to girls, but here in America I was careful what I said because no one in my class had said anything like that as far as I knew. Last winter, Nelson hadn't even known how a girl really looks down there when she's naked. He had thought girls had some sort of triangular plug hanging down between their legs. Pictures of bathing beauties in the newspaper look that way. He had never seen a real girl naked. He had only seen marble girls in the museum and in other nude pictures without a slot where girls hold their knees together.

"Cunt! Fuck! Prick! Cunt!" he shouted in Swedish as he ran around at home in his apartment before I was able to get him quiet. His married sister had been in Sweden the summer before and could hear him. I knew words in English that I didn't even know in Swedish. But I didn't say them. Not even to Nelson. He had a big mouth.

I blew water on the Japanese paper and put the wing down quickly because my hand had started to shake and I took a deep breath to make it all go away without anyone noticing.

Eloise was still standing right in front of me laughing and showing her cherub knees. But the cherub knees were just silly. Knees get like that if you try to bend your legs the wrong way, backward. Dimples and bulges appear and if the light is coming from the side they look like a face. It is about like seeing faces in water stains on carpets or in sheets of plywood if the grain is right. In the plywood walls on Äppelviken I had a whole viking head with helmet and everything to look at and fantasize about when I wanted. I had also seen cherub knees in *Life*. It had already been in several issues. People had sent in pictures of their children or brothers or sisters and everyone had cherub knees. It was like when the newspaper printed photographs of ghosts. Conan Doyle had believed in ectoplasm and things. Photographers used to fool him with various tricks. I had already read about it in *Allers* when I lived in Sweden but here *Life* acted as if it was real and printed his photographs of various ghosts.

I see Eloise standing there laughing. I see her hands, she has gathered the pleats of her skirt and is showing her knees. She has such remarkable golden skin and fine blonde down on her legs; they gleam in the light above the white knee socks. I look right at her and her skin isn't pink or white or rough and when you take her by the hand the hand is firm and warm. And I look right into her eyes. Right down into the black pupils which open as I look into them although I never usually do that or let others look into me.

It is not as if beams shine out from the eyes. It is only in picture books and comics that people draw rays coming from the eyes. But still, there is something strange about eyes. If you sit on a bus one day and look down on the street at Fifth Avenue or someplace and catch sight of someone and happen to stare, the person you're looking at never fails to turn around and look back and if you happen to look at each other your eyes lock even if you yourself are high up on a bus driving away and the other person is standing on the street. It feels about like testing with your tongue to see whether or not a flashlight battery is worn out. You feel it, not in the tongue, but in your body. It doesn't really matter whether the one you're looking at is old or young. An old lady or man or a child; they are all startled and look around to get a look at me. It is as if I had stuck them with a needle when I looked at them. And I myself notice if someone in a crowd looks at me. It is as if the observer's two black pupils of the eye grow large and visible; they shine in the middle of the crowd of small pink and brown and black and white spots of faces. It is unpleasant. That's why I'm always careful when I look at people. But I can't get myself dark glasses, although I would like to have them so I could look without others knowing what I'm looking at.

I am especially careful when it comes to looking someone directly in the eye from a short distance. That can be felt all the way down to the stomach. So I never do that. I look them in the forehead or at the tip of the nose or chin if I have to look at them as they speak. But I couldn't help it, when Eloise came I had to look her straight in the black pupils and just feel the longing. The sigh is still there, the car swings and air whistles at the window as a new freight train rattles past on its way north. Twenty small brown box cars and a few empty flatcars. And everything changes because now it has been six months since I have seen Eloise and I am sitting here at the Swedish train window again and the old men in uniform behind me are talking as they have been doing all the way from Stockholm. I can hear in their voices that they are almost forty years old. They've been called up and are going south somewhere. The one directly behind me has a tobacco shop in Sundbyberg, he says. But what the man who speaks Gothenburgese actually does I can't quite hear, except that he doesn't live in Hisingen any more, but in Bro outside Stockholm. But I do know they are drinking because I can smell it on them sometimes.

I just sit still as if I am looking out and I don't know

how their faces look because I haven't turned around one single time to look at them although the man with the tobacco shop is sitting right behind me with the others further behind. I am not listening to them and don't want to be here and I know only that two are in uniform and are soldiers because I have heard them talk about it and when I look down at the floor I can see their pants legs. They're hiding something, probably a flask, because there is a gurgling sound and one says suddenly:

"Look out. He's coming."

It was a few seconds before I heard the conductor ask whether anyone had boarded at Södertälje South. The two are drinking pure schnapps I think because it definitely smells of booze but not gin or whisky. But I don't know for sure what they're drinking and I don't know what they look like and I don't want to know. The car is full of people and the train is full of people but I haven't looked around one single time since I got on the train and rushed to find this seat and sit down. I have nothing to do with any of this. *It's none of my business.*

But the air is heavy with people behind me. They talk and mutter and sniffle and cough and chew and small children cry and it is hot and humid and smells of baby piss and people and smoke and dust and sometimes someone farts quietly beside me so I hardly want to breathe and then come whiffs of something that could be schnapps and sour beer and no one in Sweden ever wants to open a window and some old man or woman is always shouting that it's too breezy and they have rheumatism or they're afraid of catching a cold.

"Excuse me, sir, but would you mind closing the window? I'm sensitive to drafts."

I try to bring Eloise out again but as soon as her name comes to mind and I begin to get hold of her she slips away and glides off and I can't bring her out. Other thoughts come and push her aside. This freight train was the third one in an hour. We are still standing on the side track and waiting.

Straight ahead outside the sooty window there are two birches. I look down between them toward a small reedy bay in the lake which continues toward the left, far to the north, out of sight. Across the bay there is a green field beginning to turn golden with a small gray barn which is falling apart and a gray-white path leading toward the dark edge of the woods. Beyond that is a thick pine forest. It's summer and this is how Sweden looks.

Of course I have a seat although the train is packed full. I was the very first one to board the train. I didn't have any heavy luggage to check because Aunt Elsa would take care of all that after school was out when she would go down to Mariefred with her daughters, so I had arrived at Central Station in plenty of time, as she had said. But that wasn't why I had a window seat. I had that because I was first to get on the train. The others just stood there on the platform waiting like a big flock of sheep. You weren't allowed to open the gate until the train had stopped moving. So they all stood politely still and waited. People are like that in this country. It was as if those Swedes on the platform around me weren't accustomed to traveling. They just stood and stamped their feet and pushed and shoved each other without getting anywhere. But I did what I did that time in Chicago when I was on my way home to New York or what commuters did at Greenlawn. When I saw the train coming in, I got ready. I threw myself up on the step, lifted the gate and heaved my suitcase with a single swinging movement of my arm and was on board the first car before the train had even really come in. A railroad man shouted something at me but I acted as if I didn't hear him. I managed to get into the car and seat myself at the window before anyone else could get up the footsteps.

There is a certain technique for this. It was like hopping on and off streetcars in motion when I was in Stockholm before I went to America. It's just a matter of knowing when to jump and then pulling yourself up in a kind of sweeping motion. To get off, you have to start running while you're still in the air, before you land. This works, but it looks dangerous to other people. And you can't stumble, of course. It's more difficult when you have a suitcase even if it isn't especially heavy. Then you have to start by swinging the suitcase in rhythm as you get up speed and use the suitcase as a weight and swing it high enough so it helps you jump up the footstep and onto the train. You just have to keep the rhythm.

Now I'm sitting by the window with my back to the whole chock-full car and all the ladies and all the little kids and all the old drunks are behind me. I hadn't wanted to listen to the old men's chatter. They sat leaning toward each other talking quietly so they could talk in peace, but their words were still there behind me and around me and they talked mostly about the war the whole time. And they talk the way Swedes talk. No better.

France is finished, they say. Their army was just bragging. All Hitler had to do was kick them in the pants and the army ran for its life with the generals up front and then the country fell apart like a house of cards. It won't take many more days now for them to beg for mercy and give up. Too many Frenchmen died in the last war and then they took in blacks and Jews and Italians and all kinds of dagos and let them call themselves Frenchmen and the country was rotting before then anyway from corruption and whorehouses where everyone got drunk on wine even before lunchtime.

England is finished too.

"The Jews in the City will fight to the last Frenchman and when they have raked in the profits from that business, they'll move to New York," said one.

"And America," said the other. "America has only Roosevelt's crutches to offer when England asks for help. That's the only thing the Americans give away for free. England has to walk on crutches and America takes India and all the rest."

They snicker at the joke about Roosevelt's crutches. They drink some more too. Old drunks! They're Swedes! As if America was not the arsenal of the democracies! Even fifty years ago we Americans were the most powerful in the world. And I think someone really ought to turn around and tell these damned stupid Swedes, these old drunks, what our America really is. They should be forced to eat Roosevelt's crutches until the slivers stick in their throats and they fall over and roll on the floor and get blue in the face and die. But I didn't do that, of course. I just sat still with my back to them. *Sweden!*

The Germans are fools for hard work. They agree on that. But they had no sense of humor in Germany.

"If they had any sense of humor, they would have laughed so hard they would have shit in their pants, even early in the Weimar time, when little lame Goebbels talked about tall blond Aryans. And Hitler doesn't look too authentic either," said one.

But Hitler was damned effective in any case. And Goebbels was a shrewd one.

"Altogether too shrewd for my taste. A real underhanded character. Creeping and fawning like a regular Jew. And he looks like a Jewish fop from Old Town in Stockholm."

"Right. Nobody will ever know who his mother was fooling around with in the bushes. 'I have fine merchandise almost free if only beautiful Mrs. Goebbels would lift up her skirt and let me stick in my little prick,' and that's how Josef came to be," whispered the other and they both snorted with laughter.

Now they were chewing again. It smelled like cheese sandwiches. Now the one with the tobacco shop in Sundbyberg, who was sitting right behind me, said he had thought about going to Finland as a volunteer.

"But the old lady wouldn't let me. She thought I hadn't considered my obligations to her and the children. Was she supposed to run the shop all by herself? Was that my intention? she said. I told her this was no time to be so egocentric, and she should be proud to be married to a man who dared offer his life and blood for an ideal. But nothing convinced her and so the war ended before I could get away."

He leaned away now, lowered his voice, and now there was whispering behind my neck.

"She thought she knew what I really planned to do, get a little nip now and then of some horny young Finnish girl soldier. And that was true because they are good to look at and Finnish girls are a little warmer than Swedish ones. But I gave her my solemn and holy promise that such a thought had never once occurred to me since we had been married."

"Yes," said the other. "The Finland question caused a lot of trouble in many families. My older sister's son wanted to go too in place of my brother-in-law, who is an engineer in Eriksberg, but he didn't get to do it."

"Then I got called up anyway," said the one who had wanted to volunteer. "So now she can just mind the store and the kids all by herself, if you please. I'm free as a bird. Now we can maybe find out what Småland girls are like on their straw beds."

He snorted with laughter as he said this. Then I think they drank some more because a strong whiff of schnapps came from the one from Gothenburg, who was sitting behind me.

They talked about Sweden now and they both agreed that Per Albin and the Socialists were really traitors. It was their fault Sweden hadn't helped Finland. They had played games with the Russians under the covers. The Kollontai woman and the Socialists. If Sweden had really helped Finland, not deserted, but gone whole-heartedly against the Russians, then England and France and America would have done the same and then the Germans would have made peace in the west because they already had Poland and they would have gone along against the Russians and things wouldn't be the way they are. Everyone should have united to put an end to Russia instead. But Per Albin saw to it that Sweden deserted.

Babbling old men!

But those two didn't know anything about war. They had never traveled without an escort, carrying contraband through the Arctic Sea while the German U-boats *were on the prowl*. But I had. And cold salty foam came up over the bridge and froze into an icy bark and the storm whipped my face and the whole huge gray ocean tossed the MS *Mathilda Thordén* as it heaved on through the arctic storm. And that tobacconist had never been at any front, but I had. I had seen the small shit-holes down in the frozen ground which the Finns used for shelter one week and the Russians the next. I had seen their blockhouses. The lice sucked on Finns one week and on Russians the next and the frozen corpses were stacked like wood. And when I stepped down into the blockhouse the Finns had built and the Russians later captured I saw someone had carefully scratched out a huge erect penis on the left and a big open hairy cunt on the right and painted them in red and black.

"Our boys started the work," grinned the major, "and the Russians finished it and painted it, and so my heart is full. . ." He got quiet when he caught sight of me.

The wind blew across the tundra when I came out and the real film began here. They shared the lice.

Now the old Swedes behind me were gone and I put Petsamo away and the picture opened again and it was already winter up there in Minnesota, although it wasn't even Christmas yet. The captured German cannons from the Great War which stood in front of city hall had been white with frost this morning.

John and I had been out that morning walking through the small town and we stayed a long time in the square around the German cannons talking about model airplanes. He was a good builder. He was better at it than I. My hands were clumsier. Then John paced back and forth as he talked about the lecture he had been preparing all fall for the Baptist Youth Fellowship in Willmar, which was a kind of church youth club.

The pastor, whom they called a minister, had assigned John the honor of presenting a lecture at Thanksgiving on pioneer times and the whole family had been there to hear it and afterward the minister had given him special thanks. It was about the big Indian war seventy years earlier when the Sioux rose up. Only in Minnesota did they talk about the war of 1862, but it

was probably the bloodiest of all our unjust Indian wars.
It had occurred in the shadow of the great war. The Civil
War, as we said here in the North, or the War Between
the States, as they called it in the South, where they
didn't agree it was important for the future of the Union
and our development that the slave states had been lost.

John spoke to me as if I had been a whole audience
and I kept my opinions about Indian wars to myself. Mr.
Francis had debated with us in the fall about the war in
Europe and the Indian wars as well as other wars. The
Civil War for the Union against the slave states had been
a just war. China's war with Japan was a just war. The
Spanish people had waged a just war against Franco. But
he himself had been in the World War and said that war
was a typical unjust war. They had lured American boys
into going to war for the sake of big banking. Morgan
and the others had lent so much money to the British
Empire for its war that the bankers, since Russia had
made peace and the war was ending, had to bribe politicians into sending American boys to die in the mud of
Flanders so the war could continue and they could
secure the banks' insecure debts and the Indian wars
had also been totally unjustified and were only about
stealing land. And in both cases, as in the Spanish-
American War of 1898, the banks had bought off journal-
ists and poets and artists who wrote and
composed and painted so people would go along with
the war. We must not believe in wild west stories, he
said. Big railroads and other greedy profiteers stole land
from the Indians. Which we had solemnly promised they

could keep.

Mr. Francis used to say things like that in class during the late fall of 1939 when the war broke out in Europe. But he wasn't at school any more when I came home from Minnesota and winter term began. Theobald had already said in the fall that Mr. Francis was unwise and didn't have enough sense to keep his mouth shut because he knew many in our class came from important families where they didn't like such talk. There were several boys from banking families in the class. Mr. Francis was a radical, *a real Red,* and things like that didn't go well here in the *United States.* Theobald said his father was always reminding him that this was not Europe and here you had to learn to keep your thoughts quiet when strangers were nearby. And that was especially true when you hadn't been born here and could be deported as they deported people who were called Reds the last time. I understood what Theobald meant when he talked about it because I wasn't a child any more and I had also heard what others in the class said now about Reds if they didn't agree with something in the newspaper and I never contradicted them if it wasn't necessary. I just listened and thought.

Now John was walking beside me, moving back and forth in the space around the cannon speaking loudly with big gestures so people turned around to look at us and they recognized him and knew I was his cousin visiting from New York.

"It happened in the very early pioneer days as we began to cultivate the land here. Willmar had not yet been founded, that would take seven more years, and it all began down at Jackson on the Iowa state line. The crops had failed that year and it was during the Civil War so the government could not afford to give adequate rations to the Indians to keep them quiet. The pioneers were patriotic, they fought on the Union side in the war and the First Minnesota wrote an honorable page in the honor roll of the Union army. It was an heroic and honorable regiment in the war. But so many white men had gone to war that the Indians thought they were now strong enough to retake the land. The Indians also were still bitter because they had been driven out of the area. They did not understand either when we told them they had signed a treaty that said the settlers would get their land and had no respect at all for treaties and laws but continued to move around as they had always done. Several thieving Indians were caught and punished and there was trouble. Three whites were killed and then the Indians went to war under Little Crow. He was their chief. They killed five hundred whites and the settlers fled to Mankato sixty miles southwest of here. But General Sibley moved out and put them down and almost all the Sioux were either killed or driven into the wilderness to the west and the day after Christmas 1862 thirty-eight Indians were hanged. More would have been hung if President Lincoln had not been such a humanitarian. Afterward when the Indians were gone and there was peace and the Homestead Law made it possible for anyone to get land and the railroad was built we could become prosperous through honesty and hard work."

He spoke in a loud voice and with great seriousness. John and I looked very much alike although he
already wore a hat. They did that here but we New York
kids went bare-headed. I listened to him but didn't say
what I was thinking. I agreed with Mr. Francis. And the
more John talked the more I thought Mr. Francis was
right about the Indians. They had had good reasons for
going to war against the thieving pioneers. It was Sioux
land. Even the name of the state—Minnesota—was a
Sioux name.

John had given this Thanksgiving Day speech in the
Baptist church. And the whole family had been Baptist
for two generations. John himself was a believer. He had
told me that in confidence and said he might become a
missionary or go out and preach when he finished
school. He had never told anyone this before, he said.
Not even his mother. He took all this about Jesus very
seriously and meant it. John was the first boy I had met
in America who was a believer.

I hadn't contradicted him about the Indian wars and
I didn't contradict him when he talked about God either.
On the contrary, I pretended to be a believer, a Christian
and a devout one, too. We got down on our knees
beside our beds and prayed every evening as long as I
was there. The first evening when he said:

"And let us now pray!"

I did it because I didn't want to cause trouble with
him because he was Eloise's brother and she prayed
with her sisters in the evenings too. They said they were

all believers in their family and I went with them to church on Sundays. I watched Eloise as she sang and even if I didn't know whether she really believed it all I thought I could just as well go along. It didn't cost anything and none of them knew what I thought as I sat there in the pew behind her.

Later I noticed that John believed everything I said. I told him about the Bund and how they had marched and how the Bund members had been chased out of Union Square and the more I told him the more he believed. It was like Mark Twain and the story about the petrified man. He just gaped and believed and then it became exciting to see if it was possible to pretend to be pious. We fell on our knees and for me it was like walking a rope. As you balance and let yourself tip one way and then the other the people below your feet wonder how long you can keep your balance before you fall and then you wobble more and more. Especially if you're balancing on a rope high up above the floor a tickling suspense goes through your body so your mouth goes completely dry.

I took John's hand in the evening and guided him down onto his knees and when we were on our knees I made up stories about courageous missionaries and great preachers who saved many people from sin and I made up my own parables about Jesus and as I told him about the miracle of God in the human heart I shouted almost out loud from time to time: Amen! Amen! and Oh! Jesus! Oh! Jesus! and peeked at John to see if he had discovered me but he believed me the whole time and when he opened his eyes they were very bright and he told me I had been such a great help to him and he could never in his whole life have spoken so openly with anyone as he had with me about things like Christ and death and sin and faith. Not even with the pastor. And John took my hand and thanked me.

God was a story. But not an ordinary story because God was also a way for priests to live comfortably off the work of others. Grandfather and Alva were right about that. With the help of Yahweh and Christ or Baal or Krishna or whatever you called the figure you made into a god you could cheat people out of money to build churches and pay priests. The Catholic church was the very cleverest of all at this. They had installed and deposed both emperors and kings.

At Grandmother's house I had read about Catholics in Grandfather's three red volumes *Stories from a Barber-Surgeon* before I came to America where there were Jews and Catholics in my class. My last summer in Sweden I had lain on my stomach in the bright room in Mariefred and heard the words of the Jesuit and the response of the state's prisoner:

"Yes, what else!" the Jesuit began again with a sneer. "What does it matter that you, miserable tool, offer up your name, if only the church wins its great victory! What good is your earthly prize if your soul burns in the coals below, and what harm can the scorn of men cause you, if through this sacrifice you win the martyr's crown in heaven?"

"But truth...the impartial judgment of history..."

"Bah, what is history's truth? Isn't it an obedient slave, following on the heels of human error . . . a parrot, mindlessly chattering all their foolishness back to them?"

Sometimes I had thought I would come wandering to a Jesuit school and ask to become a Catholic and then a priest and then a bishop with the help of the Jesuits who saw in me the possibility of rebuilding their power and I was victorious in the College of Cardinals because of them although I hadn't thought about what I would do if I became Pope. The first thing I would do was to smash the Jesuits with clenched fist so their intrigues would be foiled for all time.

But my Catholic classmates had no such dreams. They talked about their church and their priests as if there was nothing special about them. If you were an ordinary little priest to families like these you might sit after mass on a Sunday evening after dinner and warm your stockingfeet at the wood fire and think that people were probably dumb as geese. Until there was revolution like in France when priests were forced to confess their sins before the people and tell all the people how they had cheated them of their tithes. But in America people believed in God. At least they said they did.

The funniest story I knew in Swedish about things like God was the one by August Strindberg called "The Isle of the Blessed." I had read the story time after time and laughed until I got the hiccups and my diaphragm almost hurt. Back when I first came to America in the fall of 1938 I bought Strindberg's *Swedish Fates and*

Adventures in two red volumes down at Bonnier's Scandinavian Books on 37th Street and Third Avenue. Later I found *Adamson's Journey* and *Filthy Sweden* and other books in Swedish although I had already begun reading mostly in English.

"Now let us pray!" I said to John and he fell on his knees beside me and I thought then as I prayed and got him to repeat my words that now I was Lasse who did not eat the berries of oblivion. I was a cunning Uffka who made up new prayers in the holy religion of Hell. And John was on his knees beside me with folded hands and he prayed as I told him to pray and he thanked me afterward.

I knew about ordinary Christianity in Sweden because Miss Rehn had taught me about it at Ålsten Elementary School, psalms and everything. I had had to go to church with Grandmother in Mariefred on Sundays. I knew the whole service by heart. What does the pastor say? How does the congregation answer? And I knew something about how the other Christians outside the church were when they gathered to pray because I had gone with Hans, who was also in Miss Rehn's class in Ålsten, to the Baptist church when I lived in Sweden. Hans was Baptist. He wanted to recruit me. We had sat in the brown pews on the right-hand side and I had watched them and listened to them and pretended a little so Hans wouldn't be uncomfortable because he had taken me along.

"So you've been visiting the natives," said Gunnar when I told him about it. "Did they stick you in a big pot too?" and he laughed.

But he said that only because he was in a good mood and Alva didn't hear him and he had said it himself. Otherwise you could never say anything about Christians without hearing about showing respect for other people and their beliefs. Alva said you always have to be careful and hold your tongue and you should never show what you're thinking when you meet pastors or the rabbis they have in America including the fathers of some of my classmates. Especially not in America. Here you always have to think before you speak.

That was why it was particularly exciting to see how long I could keep John going. I made up various Christian adventures and confessed to him and told him how I had disappointed my Lord Jesus when my unbelieving classmates at school in Sweden wanted to beat me because I was a believer and I betrayed my faith out of cowardice but later stayed on my knees the whole night and begged Gentle Lord Jesus for forgiveness until I felt his grace. And John believed it! It showed in his eyes and his open mouth.

I understood how pastors felt when they got control of their congregations. They did what I did with John and it was enormously exciting. It was a matter of who was stronger and was like wrestling except you only used words and intonations and gestures and expressions and things. I had read about how it was done. Both in Hunt's little green book about hypnotism and suggestions which I had taken from Alva's bookshelf and in the novel about Elmer Gantry.

I never told John I was doing all this with him only in fun. Because really it was not just a game in which I tested how long I could string him along. This way I could stay with them a while longer although otherwise I was supposed to go to Great Uncle Albert and the other relatives in St. Paul. I wanted to be in the same house with Eloise. I wanted to go with Eloise to visit her friends. So I had to get all of them to think well of me. And when Eloise wasn't looking I watched her and at night I thought about her that way. But I didn't say anything to John. I never talked with him about his sister. I just acted with him and his whole family as if it were he and I who were good really good friends although I felt indifferent toward him and thought he was rather dumb although he was good at building model airplanes.

I could make use of him in other ways as well. You can't act out scenes very well by yourself. After Christmas when I had been with them a while we acted out the raid on Harper's Ferry with John's tin soldiers. But first we had a meeting up in Canada where I appointed myself commander in chief and dictator and John had to help me write the Provisional Constitution and Ordinances for the new government under which all slaves would be free. After we had lost and ten of my men had fallen I was too proud to flee so John had to be Robert E. Lee and ask John Brown what right he had to take up weapons and I stood in the middle of the floor with right arm outstretched and index finger raised into the air and tears almost came to my eyes as I said with as thunderous a voice as possible:

"To free the slaves with the authority of God Almighty!"

Then we took turns reading John Brown's speech in court because John wanted to read too although I read better. Great-uncle Albert had told him that this speech was almost as important as the Gettysburg Address.

When John Brown was finally about to be hanged he walked to the gallows on his own and put the noose around his neck and died with dignity so people would remember him for time and eternity.

But the day we played John Brown and I felt the words throughout my whole body I discovered nothing happened to John. It was as if he hadn't heard the words within himself. He just said he was hungry. I should have thought about that and understood. But I didn't do that because I played with him for the sake of Eloise. After lunch we sat in his den, his lair, as usual. It was a kind of small gentleman's room or little office. The girls in the family all slept in the same bed in the same room but John was a boy and would carry on the name and because of that he not only had his own room for sleeping but also his den. A special room, his own lair, where he could build model airplanes and do homework and listen to the radio. Sometimes one of the sisters came in to visit. I waited for Eloise to come. When she stood in the doorway I felt myself turn red and at first didn't dare look her in the eyes although I wanted to.

And now I don't think about John and remember only Eloise and now as I stare at the reedy bay and the edge of the woods it hurts and there is a clump in my chest and my eyes sting because she's standing in front of me in her tight turtleneck sweater and her gray skirt and says:

"See, I have cherub knees too."

But just as I hear her say that and this time really try to look her right in the eyes I see her eyes get stern. Now they're black with disdain and I hear her voice as she talks about the *new davenport* and then behind me John starts to talk about Jesus Christ and duty and sacrifice and *the mission* again and I can't see Eloise very well any more because she's lost her color and voice. John's voice becomes almost Swedish and I can see only the gray barn across the bay in the middle of the landscape outside the window and now the old schnapps men are talking about the arson in Luleå. But they don't call it arson.

"It's too bad about the boys. They just wanted to get rid of the damn Communist paper and so they blew the whole house up and ended up killing the whole commie family including the brats. But they didn't mean to. It just happened. Anyway, the paper was shut down. Sure, maybe the authorities had to take it to court and make a case of it now the way things went with people dying and all. But I can't help thinking it's a little legalistic to treat them that way. And it must have been hard for the judge to convict them. They only did it out of patriotism."

"They didn't handle it right. No one should find out if you do. They couldn't have done it right. They got caught. Officers shouldn't be so stupid that they get captured like a snot-nosed kid with a hand in the jam jar."

Now I think they ate again because they were quiet for a while. But I heard paper rustle and then there was chewing very close beside me. They drank some more too. After a while the old men picked up their conversation again and I couldn't think their voices away.

"They could just as well have kept quiet about Communists up there and not given them extra publicity. No, they should have shut down the newspapers and locked the Communists in a camp somewhere and then taken them out on the ice and beat them on the head with a club in the night and stuck them in a hole in the ice and just let them disappear and put a lid on all the talk and this whole thing would never have become a big story."

"There would have been talk even then. Someone always blabs."

The voices press toward me the whole time although I try to close my ears. Old Swedish drunks, I think. God damn old Swedish drunks to Hell. I form the words on my lips but don't let out a sound. I stare out through the window and try to build a wall between me and the old men and old ladies and kids and their eating and talking and bickering and their piss odor. But Eloise is gone and her picture won't open in front of me no matter how hard I try. The barn is just as broken-down out there, coal smoke sticks in my nose and the old men's voices come through the whole time. And it's just as if they were Chicago Legionnaires.

"They should have done it right. They could have

sent them across the border and let the Finns take charge of them and then say they ran off when it began to smell like cats up there and they probably crossed the eastern border on their way to their real homeland and then no one would know anything."

"But the boys weren't rational. They were overexcited. Just young punks. They weren't thinking."

"The police superintendent who took part should be excused for his stupidity because he was insane, you mean. Sure! But when the whole thing came out and there was a scandal something had to be done. They had to be convicted of something. It should have been handled another way. I could have done it myself with my left hand."

Now the train jumps. Those old men must have drunk a whole lot because they shout with laughter and the tobacconist from Sundbyberg yells at the top of his lungs:

"Lock your doors and gates, good people."

The coupling chains rattle and the bumpers crash into each other. There is puffing and slamming and shaking and pulling and slowly the train gets up speed and the barn is gone and now the scene is changing outside the streaked window and the lake out there disappears and later there are pine forests again and only pine forests and I can't hear so well any more what they're saying behind me because the train leans and there is screeching and knocking in the old car's woodwork, and there is thumping in the rails and outside the windows Sweden passes by.

CHAPTER 5

The landscape closed in darkly around our wobbling train. Now the sky was barely visible. The forest grew tall. The pines stood so close to the railroad bed that they almost scraped the dirt-streaked windows. There are no real trains in Sweden. In America we had them. It was uncomfortable to sit the way I sat and there were puffs of coal smoke and the old Swedish train groaned and leaned and rocked as it moved south very slowly through the pine forest. I supposed the reason it moved so slowly was the war and mobilization traffic. That was what blocked stretches of track. And there was probably also military traffic that took all the good cars so we here in this train had to sit in these miserable and life-endangering wooden cars. At a cornfield meet they'd be smashed to kindling and we'd all die. The locomotive wasn't much to talk about. I don't know the Swedish locomotives very well and I hadn't been able to look closely but I think this locomotive was pretty decent, an older passenger locomotive litt. B. from 1910, a 2'C as they said or a 4-6-0, a Ten-Wheeler, as we would have said. It works with a much lower steam pressure than our real locomotives in America and isn't especially heavy but can be used on small tracks like these here. Maybe it had been in storage.

Last winter it was different! The 480 miles from

Chicago to St. Paul and the 480 miles back to Chicago I had traveled on the Chicago, Milwaukee, St. Paul and Pacific, on something completely different, on a real train for the twentieth century, their "Hiawatha." The name of the railroad was entirely too long so the train was usually called simply "The Milwaukee Road." And the real Hiawatha had been one of the Indians' greatest statesmen 400 years ago. What Longfellow wrote about him was just fiction. But Longfellow was pretty boring in other ways too. He was someone I did not read. In school they had told us about the real Hiawatha. The one who had organized the Iroquois league, which later became the Six Nations. We had deceived them and cheated them and taken their land away and Barbara had sat both classes in a circle on the floor and she sat cross-legged in the middle of the circle. She had closed her eyes and swayed and beat the drum with the flat of her hand and we had sung after her:

> Woe! Woe!
> Hearken ye!
> We are diminished!
> The cleared land has become a thicket.
> Woe! Woe!
> The clear places are deserted.
> Woe!
> They are in their graves —
> They who established it —
> Woe!
> The great League.

Yet they declared
It should endure —
The great League.
Woe!
Their work has grown old.
Woe!
Thus we are become miserable.

When the song was over she remained sitting there in the middle of the circle and closed her eyes and swayed and hummed as she continued to drum with the flat of her hand and finally my eyes began to water and I felt sniffles coming on and I began to cry although everyone could see. On the way home Nelson and I talked about everything that had happened in school that day except just that. I think he almost cried too.

The Hiawatha train was probably the most famous in the world. There had been just six streamlined cars in the train a few years before when they had started to run it express. There were now twelve cars and almost 600 passengers when I came down on the train that left for Chicago at one in the afternoon. Because there were so many passengers and therefore so many cars they had doubled the train and changed from the Atlantic locomotive to the more powerful Hudson and gone from a 4-4-2 to a 4-6-4 although the oil-powered Atlantic locomotive is actually more beautiful and more popular with engineers.

I had sat way in the back of the observation car coming up on "The Morning Hiawatha" and knew that the fastest steam engine in the world, a coal-powered and streamlined Class F-7 in the 100-series just built by Alco, was pulling the train. According to the schedule we were doing 80 miles an hour. But we could go 100 miles an hour if necessary and the train had been clocked at 125 miles an hour. And the train was carrying a full load. Nowhere else in the world was there such a fast steam engine. I had been up front and looked at it. Although it had one of those streamlined hoods, it was a pure classic. I knew its specifications. Fifty feet long, the fire box was eight feet by twelve feet, seven feet in diameter at the high driving gear and Walschaerts slide-valve steering and a real tender with two three-axled bogies. There was room for enough coal and water and then some.

Actually I didn't like it when they put streamlined hoods on locomotives. It was not an essential part of the design. Even the machinery was offended. Steam engines lost their own beauty that way. They looked cheap like girls with too much make-up. Dressed-up locomotives from various railroads had been exhibited in the railroad section of the World's Fair. They had told me and other visitors there that NYC's Hudson had been styled by Henry Dreyfuss and that the world's largest and heaviest steam locomotive which weighed 526 tons and had been designed by Pennsylvania's engineers—a 6-4-4-6—had been styled by Raymond Loewy. But they didn't say who the engineers were. That had irritated me.

At the World's Fair I had also seen the English streamlined ,hooded Coronation engine. They had driven it around America and then put it on exhibit. It was their pride. A Pacific locomotive, 4-6-2. But in spite of everything it couldn't compare with the Hiawatha's Hudson. It was 20 feet shorter and two feet lower and almost 90 tons lighter. A locomotive which suited a little island off Europe. But its design was finer and it had much higher steam pressure than anything in Sweden, of course. Here they hadn't been keeping up with developments. Locomotive steam pressure is still at a nineteenth century level. And here in Sweden where they knew nothing about the Hiawatha's Hudson, the general directors and railroad engineers and stationmasters and others at the State Railroad probably didn't know there were things like the English Coronation locomotive out in the world.

And the darkness out there, which sprawled and spread close by the windows, is Sweden. Spruce Sweden. The old men are quiet now. They're sleeping. And those who hiss and wheeze behind me, those who snort and snore, are this dark needled land's natives. The Swedish people.

> The Swedish people are a farting people
> Oh, yes, a farting people.
> Sweden is a dark old land
> Oh, yes, a dark old land.

> Svenska folket är ett fisande folk
> Oh ja, ett fisande folk.
> Sverige är ett mörksens land
> Oh ja, ett mörksens land.

Yes, I sat by the window in a Swedish wooden train with open platforms. Four thumping iron wheels and a woodbox. No real couplings even. Like in the nineteenth century. And this was what they called a main line in Sweden!

Do you call that a train?
No! No!
Do you call that a train, brother?
Oh no! No never!

The rhythm behind it was the important thing. On that you embroider words, as the younger Lomax said at the music lecture in school when he introduced Huddie Ledbetter, Leadbelly. Mrs. Roosevelt was the one who got him out of prison. My class and several other classes were working on rural folkways. Leadbelly sang for us then. He sang "Boll Weevil" and "Pick a Bale of Cotton" and talked about them. He finished with "Midnight Special" and at *"shine its everloving light on me"* I had to clench my teeth his voice hurt so much.

Afterward in music hour we had to stand in a line and clap our hands and sing *"Pick a Bale of Cotton"* while different pairs danced. But I didn't want to dance. I wasn't good at it. Then we sat on the floor and talked about the cotton economy and *sharecropping* and looked at photographs. Barbara, who was in charge of music, was a student at Columbia and spent a lot of time on the kind of Southern music that reflects the rural economy because that's what she was writing about in her dissertation. But she also had us sing *street songs*. Barbara herself was from the Lower East Side and that was why she knew all the songs girls sang there when they jumped rope or bounced balls. Most of the class had never played in the street and were a little uncertain when she positioned herself right in front of the class and said:

"Just you sing after me!"

Then she put her hands on her hips and sang out loud and at every phrase she made a final jerk with her lower body so her skirt wrapped around her and we sang:

> *The prettiest girl*
> > *The prettiest girl*
> *I ever met*
> > *I ever met*
> *pushed ten kids*
> > *pushed ten kids*
> *in a cart*
> > *in a cart*
> *down Third Avenue.*
> > *down Third Avenue.*
> *Seven were her own*
> > *Seven were her own*
> *and three her ma's.*
> > *and three her ma's.*
> *And she said:*
> > *And she said:*
> *They just keep a-coming!*
> > *They just keep a-coming!*

Many of the street songs she sang for us when she bounced a ball or jumped rope were almost dirty. Not the words themselves maybe but especially the way she sang with both her voice and her body word by word:

She has oomph,
she has it,
she can do the splits,
but you bet
she will never do this!

It was also she who told us that nursery rhymes and children's games are some of the oldest cultural artifacts.

"When you count somebody out by pointing and counting: Eenie, meeney, miney, mo, you're using the oldest Welsh tribe's counting words."

She was one of the teachers I thought about sometimes at night. She was like Karna had been. The same age too. The way she stood. And the expression on her mouth. But the opposite in some ways. They were both very much alike and very different. But she brought Lomax and Leadbelly to school.

I was assigned to give a talk on the background of "The Boll Weevil Holler." The boll weevil is one of the most destructive insects we have. It is a gray-brown beetle about a quarter of an inch long. Anthonomus grandis is its name. In Swedish it would be "Bomullsvivel," cotton weevil. It comes from Central America and reached Texas in 1892. Since 1922 it has taken over all our cotton fields and we now lose an average of 1.5 million bales of cotton each year due to its ravages. In the discussion afterward she sang the song for us very distinctly so we could hear every word:

"There's a double meaning in the next," she said. "Do you understand?"

The song was not only about an insect, she said, it was also about the whole life situation of the sharecroppers. The boll weevil represented the life of landowners as well as merchants and bankers. It was actually a song of *social protest*. "Pick a Bale of Cotton" on the other hand was a proud song. In it working people danced at the end of the day with pride in their work.

I liked "Gray Goose" best because there was something that didn't quite fit in "Pick a bale of cotton." You can't just jump down turn around and pick a bale a day. Sterling A. Brown had told me when he was out at our house on Long Island that it's impossible to pick a bale of cotton in one day and that it was questionable whether it was even a genuine reel that one danced to in the evenings. He thought it was probably a song mostly made for white audiences. But "Gray Goose" was a real folk song. It was about a goose no one could kill. You could shoot it and pluck it and cook it for six weeks but whenever you tried to slice it you couldn't and if you took the goose to the sawmill the saw broke its teeth on it and Sterling sang:

> *And the last time I seed him*
> *He was flying across the ocean*
> *with a long string of goslings*
> *And they were all going: "Quink, Quack.*

Despite everything that had been done to the gray goose, he thought no white Southerner could really like hearing that they were all going: "Quink, Quack." I try letting the thumping of the rails set a rhythm and embroidering words on it like Leadbelly with "Gray Goose" or maybe "Midnight Special," which is more the way I'm feeling just now *(Oh you wake up in the morning, hear the ding-dong ring. Go marching to the table, see the same damn thing)* and look out at the spruce forest going by and sing softly to myself so no one can hear and interfere with the words. But now that the train has worked up a little speed the rhythm doesn't work any more. They have such short rails in this country. And we haven't had cars like these since the Civil War. Yes, on our small *narrow-gauge lines* in the South and *far out West* there were cars like this.

There is snoring around me because the old drunks are sleeping. The one in the middle is sniffling with an open mouth I see now that I can look at him. The one beside me is like a heavy sack of hay against me. I shove him with my elbow so he leans in the other direction and I notice how he rolls over and outside there is only forest and forest and forest.

And they can't even build things so they last, these Swedes. We're coming to Getå soon. There the roadbed gave way under the express train from Malmö at seven in the morning October 1, 1918. It was built of clay and white sand and when the locomotive had beat long enough on the roadbed and the rain came, the roadbed slipped and everything began to slide toward Bråviken.

The Swedish engineers had forgotten that there had been an ice age in this country and that in the following geological period it rained every autumn and white sand turned to soap.

In this autumn Swedish morning darkness the locomotive derailed and seven cars went down the incline and started to burn. Forty-one people died down there under the landslide that morning. It was no accident. It was the stupidity of the engineers. There are really no accidents. "Accident" is only one of those words only ignorant people use. A few weeks ago there were complaints at home on the radio and in the newspaper because there had been a crash in the night for the Lake Shore Limited on the Chicago run up in the Mohawk Valley on the New York Central system. It was no accident! The roadbed wasn't as poorly built as the one at Getå but the curve there is the worst on the line. The express was fifteen minutes late. Engineer Jesse Earl tried to make up time and *was hitting sixty miles an hour* when he went into the curve. That was fifteen miles an hour over the limit and his locomotive jumped the track and *nine cars piled up* and thirty people died and a hundred were injured. The spruce trees rattled by and now the train sang:

> *Put in your water and shovel in your coal*
> *Put your head out the window, watch them*
> *drivers roll*
> *I'll run her till she leaves the rail*
> *'Cause I'm a quarter of an hour late with that*

Chicago mail
He looked at his watch and the watch was slow,
He looked at the water and the water was low,
He turned to the fireman and then he said:
"We're goin' to reach Chicago but we'll all be
*   dead!"*

If that was an accident then I'm Mary Mother of Christ! You don't need to be a trained railroad engineer to know what happens when you take a train into a curve with too much speed. You only need to have played with a toy train. There are no accidents. There is only stupidity and intentional violations. Gunnar used to say that. Anyone who hits his own thumb with a hammer wants to hit his thumb. Otherwise he would not have held out his thumb and hit it, he used to say if someone complained.

Talk of misfortune is one of the coward's consciously ignorant excuses, he said at Sunday dinner during a discussion about why I first broke the fine china ashtray when I was wiping it and then said it was an accident. It was slippery after washing and I lost my grip on it and that was why it fell, I said apologizing. That was an excuse, he thought. I should have asked myself instead why I had wanted to break the ashtray. There were very few things he cared about in this life, I knew that. But I had known that this particular ashtray meant a lot to him. His students in Geneva had presented it to him as a farewell gift the first time he was a professor, he said. It was important to him. Therefore, I should realize and understand that I had broken the ashtray to take revenge on him. Dropping the ashtray was actually an act of rebellion toward my father. It is only with this kind of insight into yourself and seeing your motives clearly that you can become a person, he said. And if you say when something happens that it just is that way then you are deceiving yourself, keeping yourself at a sub-human level and in unconsciousness and can never grow into a worthwhile person. Fingers slip because you yourself decided they would slip. No excuses, then! he said. And Alva agreed. Only she said it in French, he who excuses himself accuses himself.

There is always someone who bears responsibility. So you would have to ask the track engineer who designed the eastern branch line why he planned the Getå catastrophe. But he was probably dead when it happened. I looked out into the dark forest as it passed by and made an animated film about it all:

A little man with bald head and eyeglasses sits at his drawing board at the railroad's central office and just waits and you see how his fat fingers with big gold rings on them drum on the empty surface. He chuckled and chuckled. And it went on that way until fall 1918 when he himself had just retired and then died before the plans were carried out and the mass murder plot realized. But it was difficult to show. You must say that.

But you could have a calendar or something lose its pages and years and it all falls down around him like snow while he is made up to look older and older. Then you would have shown that he sat there at his empty drawing table with his high white collar all those years waiting and on the wall behind him a row of portraits in oil paint with gold oval frames. There hung all his criminal predecessors with white muttonchop beards and large medals on their chests. And I saw how the film showed the railroadbed sliding, the white sand now slippery as soap after the big rain and the locomotive falls and drags the cars after it and flames reach high into the heavens and the criminal chief engineers turn their oil-painted heads toward each other and chuckle so the medals jump.

Now water appears. The old men have awakened. They talk about girls. The one from Sundbyberg leans forward and whispers so they both giggle. He tells about how he had been with his wife's sister when the wife had just come home after having a baby and couldn't do it yet:

"The coffee rolls are almost done," she called out. "And then when she bent down I just lifted her skirt and took her from behind right there as she stood at the baking table. She gasped a little then but the wife didn't notice a thing."

All at once I see Eloise again. But now we are at a party and I am already getting sick. And of course I know why. And of course I know why I tried to focus all my thoughts and what I saw of her cherub knees.

"On the new davenport!"

In the middle of the party she had taken me to and with all her friends there I stood and vomited all over the carpet and I vomited on the fine desk and everyone just looked at me with disgust and I heard her words:

"On the new davenport."

John hadn't been allowed to come along to the party. He was too small although he was just one year younger. But he had stood in the doorway and sneered when I went to the party with the dressed-up Eloise because he knew what would happen.

I had felt it coming when we started to dance. Yes, I had felt it from the beginning when I came into the warmth of the house after having walked there with Eloise. But I had persuaded myself I would make it. It was her best friend's birthday and she had invited her classmates. Eloise had been allowed to take me along, her cousin from New York. But John had not been allowed to go. He was too young, said Eloise at lunch.

What happened was my own fault. And I had known what would happen before I changed clothes to go with Eloise to the party.

That afternoon John had *dared me*. Earlier, one of my first days, I had said I could drink ink and eat soap. Yes, I could chew apart a drinking glass and swallow the pieces too if I got mashed potatoes to eat afterward.

"It's not dangerous," I had said. "It's like swallowing fire. It looks dangerous but it's only a matter of knowing how."

He began to talk about that again that afternoon right after lunch. He had seen sword-swallowers and fire-eaters at the circus that had come through Willmar in the fall. I had said that I did indeed know how to eat fire, you just had to blow out and then pinch your

mouth right to put out the flame but I was going to learn
to be a real sword swallower. It would be swell to be
able to do that. Then he had taken a bar of green soap
from his pocket:

"I bet you can't eat this up," he said.

"Sure I can," I said.

The soap looked sticky and unappetizing and I
knew John had had it in his pocket since just after lunch.

"You don't dare!" said John.

"Yes I do," I said. "But that's an old dirty soap."

"I can clean it up," he said. He washed the soap
well under the faucet in the bathroom and held it out to
me again.

"But you don't dare," he said and looked me right
in the eyes.

Then I ate it up. I could do nothing else because he
dared me. But it was slimy and repulsive and tasted bad.
Maybe John thought I wasn't going to chew and swallow
the whole bar of soap. Maybe he thought I was just
bragging and that I would get sick right away. But I
didn't because I saw on his face that he was just waiting
for that. I chewed the disgusting soap and swallowed the
bad-tasting mush that filled my mouth although I
belched time after time.

The whole rest of the afternoon he talked to me
about Jesus. He told how he wanted to go as a missionary to the Indians in Peru. And he wondered about my
plans for the future, would I really spread the word as I
had said? I saw in his eyes that he was really just waiting
for me to get sick from the soap I had eaten and for me

to start throwing up. But I restrained myself.

Now as I stood vomiting in the middle of the room with Eloise's friends all dressed up around me and the host, the father of Eloise's best friend, took my arm and led me out as one leads a puppy who has thrown up on the rug, I thought John had taken revenge on me. It had started to snow. Eloise had had to leave the party to take me home. She didn't say anything to me.

The next day I took the bus to St. Paul and Great-Uncle Albert. Eloise hardly looked at me when I said goodbye to the family. I don't know whether John said anything to them about me which was repeated to Great-Uncle Albert but I think he did because the evening before I was supposed to go on to Chicago Great-Uncle Albert was very serious and called me into his room just before dinner. He sat down on a chair beside the window and took out the Bible. He laid it on the little white table. There was no chair for me, I had to stand in front of him. For a moment he sat silently with his head bowed and folded his old man's hands and I knew that he was praying. He looked at me as I stood there and began to speak to me:

"I want to ask you Jan what your relationship with God is like, but your father ought to do that. When he was young and visited here he was God-fearing, he like his father, your grandfather, my brother Adolf, even if they did like to sing and play and brother Adolf had his trials here in life as do we all. I don't think your father forgot his God although he's successful now in this worldly life. But if your grandfather were still with us he would have spoken with you now.

"I want to tell you something which will be useful for you to hear now that you are no longer a child. What I will tell you is something which has given me strength over the years. When Johan and I were going to leave Solvarbo and move to America to work and make our futures, father said now that we were leaving Myres and we might never see each other again in this life, mother had asked us to come and bring our little brother Adolf into the house because she had a few words for us from both of them.

"What she said next I have always borne in my heart and you ought to know that those words were also said for you because it was your great-grandmother speaking and she spoke for your great-grandfather and you belong to a God-fearing family. She said: 'I give you heart-felt blessings from me and your father on your departure and may God keep you and protect you and give you happiness and blessings and above all give you his peace which the world can never give and may he keep you with him for blessed are those who belong to the Lord God. It is happiness here on earth to belong to the Lord and there is such blessed hope for eternity in the heavenly home above. I have wanted to tell you this from father and me because it is uncertain that we will see each other again down here, but whatever happens to us, earthly life is short and fleeting but may God guide us so we may be near him always and meet again above.

" 'And remember on your way through life,' she continued to say to us, 'that the Lord delivers the God-

fearing from temptation but the Lord will capture and
punish on Judgment Day those who do not respect God
and, in truth, those who seek after the flesh with impure
desires and self-satisfied defiant ones who despise the
Lord's kingdom. With that your father and I as your parents bless you and admonish you to think constantly of
God for eternity.'

"Mother had tears in her eyes as they blessed us
and we three brothers all wept and I have never forgotten her words and I know that brother Adolf will never
forget them either no matter what life brings.

"It is good even for you Jan to hear these words so
you know where you belong. For," he said as he picked
up the Bible, opened it, searched a short time and began
to read and now he read in English:

"As a madman who casteth firebrands, arrows and
death, so is the man that deceiveth his neighbor, and
saith, Am I not in sport?"

He grew quiet and stared at me. I stood still in front
of him without saying anything and when he had looked
silently at me for a long moment he laid the Bible down,
bowed his head and folded his hands and I knew he
was going to pray again.

Then it was over. Great-Uncle Albert got up from
the chair and laid his hand on my shoulder and we went
into the living room where the others were waiting for
us before going to the table in the dining room. They
didn't talk about what had happened in Willmar and
although they conversed with each other they didn't say
anything special to me but asked me to greet my father

and mother and sisters from them and my farewell meal was turkey with real wild rice. The kind of native American rice that grows wild here in the northern United States and Canada and that the Indians harvest.

"Don't forget what I said," said Great-Uncle Albert in the hall when we said goodbye and I shook his hand and bowed and said:

"No, I won't."

Then he gave me a black American Bible with a soft cover and gilt edges and said:

"Take this book as a present. A more precious gift you can never receive. I have written the same words in this one as my father wrote in my first Bible and your grandfather wrote in your father's confirmation Bible because that's our custom."

I bowed and shook his hand one more time and already knew before I opened the Bible to look at what he had written. It was the words of the preacher about how through sloth the roof sinks in, and through indolence the house leaks, as Gunnar used to read to me. Ecclesiastes 10:18 the passage would be called in English. But that wasn't it. Great-Uncle Albert had written instead: *To Jan. Remember I Corinthians 16:13:*

Watch ye, stand fast in the faith, quit you like men. Be strong.

But I knew this verse in Swedish too because Miss Rehn had taught it to us and I had used it when I wanted to make John get on his knees and pray:

Vaken, stån fasta i tron, varen män, varen starka.

Then I departed. Great-Uncle Albert's second son gave me a ride to the station.

But on the Hiawatha to Chicago I thought I saw the words Great-Uncle Albert had said to me written on a big blackboard and I stood in front of the blackboard and erased them one after the other until they were all gone. And if John hadn't dared me it wouldn't have gone so badly at the party and if he hadn't squealed I wouldn't have been sent to Great-Uncle Albert. But that's the way John was. *A creep! A mealy-mouthed son-of-a-bitch preacher soul!* A real Jesuitical would-be black-coat.

The old men here beside me were still talking about girls. But now they whispered so quietly to each other that I could hear almost nothing except their snickers. Snickering drunks! We had already passed Getå and I saw the conductor coming.

"Next stop Karlsro," he called from the doorway. Then he came all the way up to me and said:

"Here is where you get off."

But when I got up and went out to the platform I felt it would be impossible to think about Eloise anymore because I saw myself stand vomiting in front of her and all of Great-Uncle Albert's words had appeared on the blackboard again and first I felt myself throwing up from the soap and then all at once deep in my spinal cord I felt the shame as horribly as I had felt it standing there in front of Great-Uncle Albert listening to him talk.

CHAPTER 6

In three weeks I would be thirteen years old and they were on their way back to America. They were going to leave me in this Hitler Sweden while they traveled home to New York.

It was late morning in not-at-war Sweden and the air was still. Thunderstorms were already threatening and I dragged the heavy rake across the huge driveway in front of the manor house. Midsummer was past and France had fallen before the French army was able to organize a counter-attack and proper defense, except against Italy, of course. Marshall Pétain had formed a capitulation government in the south and his government which had surrendered France had just left Bordeaux and gone into the country toward Clermont-Ferrand, it said in the newspapers. The Russians had taken the Baltics and the war on the Continent was over and Germany's soldiers had been victorious on all fronts and Hitler had humbly thanked God for these blessings it said in the newspapers and now churchbells were ringing joyously throughout Germany for the seventh day.

It was Sunday and morning and here in this Sweden which Hitler could take precisely when he wanted because the Swedes would never defend themselves at all but do as the Danes had done, mark my words! here the pastors certainly hadn't dared proclaim a day of celebration because the Huns ruled the European continent but they let the churchbells ring and the bishops in this country had declared a day of spiritual preparation and I thought about the cowardice of the pitiful Swedish black-coats and I dragged the rake under the lindens. Gravel rolled between my toes. I was barefoot but I liked it because the soles of my feet were already hard, I could walk on the stubbled fields if necessary. The driveway was long and I dragged the heavy ironclad wood rake behind me and high above a cloud appeared to grow. It rose slowly now over the roof of the house. I America we had other preachers than the Danes and the Swedes and the French, we had real men of God.

And now I heard a song behind me as I dragged the rake:

"He's gone to be a soldier in the army of the Lord."

But there were people like that only at home and w were the ones who would wring Hitler's neck.

The cloud had risen even higher above the roof, already filling half the eastern sky. I was living this summer of 1940 with Uncle Robert and Aunt Greta at Marieborg outside Norrköping, as agreed by the family. It was in a manor at Bråviken which had been made into a folk high school. Robert was director now and wanted to do things the folk high school way. Laughing and thumping you on the back. He was comradely like a young Elmer Gantry I thought. But without being religious or anything. And he was thinner than Elmer Gantry would have been at this age. In any case he was no Nazi sympathizer. He couldn't stand Hitler and his hangers-on. He spoke well of our president even if he didn't know much about our politics. If he had been a friend of Germany I would have left. He was just a little foolishly comradely and busy like our Y.M.C.A. leader used to be.

"Poor Robert goes through life like an assistant pastor in a difficult parish where he's afraid the people will start to smear chicken blood on his nose all of a sudden," Gunnar had said and thought I hadn't understood a thing.

But I didn't say that here, of course. Maybe they hadn't read *Elmer Gantry* here in Sweden anyway although *Falstaff Fakir* in a five-volume popular edition stood on the bookshelf up in the school library. Aunt Greta on the other hand had sharp eyes. And if Robert was rather weak Greta was a real pointy-nosed shrew. That's what Gunnar had said. But not so Alva heard. When he started to say things like that Alva always began talking about something else. She was afraid I would hear. Or the housekeeper. Or the conductor, waiter, messenger, doorman, elevator boy, mailman. Or the guests in the next hotel room. But Gunnar was certainly right. Greta was one of those aunts you could read about in old books for boys. A shrew.

Grandmother lived here too during the summer. She would take care of the children. She was older now than I remembered her. All the cousins had gathered here at Marieborg. But they were all much younger than I.

There had been porridge for breakfast as usual. We cousins ate it in the big student dining room. Aunt Greta had been standing in the doorway when I came down, she had inspected my hands and checked to see that I was clean around the neck. You had to be scrubbed pink to pass. I didn't pass that morning either. I had to turn around and leave the dining room. I had to clean my fingernails one more time and wash myself better before I could sit at the table again. I wore short pants and was always barefoot except when I was going into Norrköping because going barefoot was good for you. And in the evenings Aunt Greta checked to see that my feet were clean and that I was clean between the toes before I could get under the sheets.

Outside the glass doors to the dining room, toward the garden, was the same gray-green thin Sweden down at Bråviken as there had been the day before and the day before that and last week and the week before that. But the heat was already oppressive and there was thunder from below the horizon, flies buzzed and the haze thickened. But this didn't really matter because when I wanted to get away, I could, look closely and strain my eyes and see the true reality behind. But I never told them I could do this. It was like with the pictures.

I was only present here as long as I didn't want to do anything else. But I never say that. You should never let them find out you're different. There were no eggs on the table. Eggs were not healthy. *Cereals* weren't healthy either. I had brought two packages of Kellogg's Pep to Marieborg. They were real breakfast flakes. Like we ate in America but did not exist in Sweden. Thirty percent bran it said on the package and you could feel it between your teeth! And full of vitamins. This kind of breakfast could really wake you up. Full of *zest*. The Irishwoman had been the first to eat Kellogg's Pep. Maybe because she was constipated. In any case it was a good breakfast. But Greta had taken my packages away. It didn't look right for me to have special food. I should eat porridge like all the others. What she did with them I don't know. Maybe she and Robert sat and munched secretly on Kellogg's Pep with 30 percent bran. To cure constipation. Then they each sat on a toilet and shat. Maybe. I had also brought a package along from America for making real butterscotch pudding. But Aunt Greta didn't know about that; I had hid that package. If she got hold of it she would only say if you didn't use a pint of milk but several liters of milk when you cooked the pudding, then everyone could have some. And it wasn't that I was miserly. I could imagine cooking it the way it should be cooked and sharing it so we would each get only a little dab of pudding. But I wanted what we got to be right, with the right color and the right consistency and taste like it's supposed to have. They didn't understand that. So I hid the package.

The little cousins around me made smacking noises when they ate. I sat with porridge in front of me and thanked God that I had regained my sight because yesterday I couldn't see any butter or cheese on the bread, but today I can see the bowl through the milk. But if I said that so Greta could hear I would be arrogant and upper-class and besides didn't I know there was a war on and how did I think French children had it now with

German troops occupying their country? I saw her standing in the doorway watching us and I knew every word
she would say to me if I told her what I was thinking.
Most of the time I didn't have to talk to any of them, I
knew in advance and could hear everything that would
be said. Could just as well yawn and be quiet. My little
sisters laughed and screamed. The cousins pounded on
the table with their spoons. And for one short moment I
had made them go away. I made them disappear. It
looked strange, first they became like net curtains and
then completely transparent and then they floated away
sort of like cigar smoke. And the room had grown very
quiet. After that I lifted up the walls and saw the beach
on Long Island Sound again, beyond the trees. I took a
year out of time. Cut it out, threw it in the wastebasket
and turned July 1939 into the present the way they do
when they edit films. I backed up a little and began
rolling it forward. Back there in reality it was still a dark
thundering night and lightning flashed across the sky
and struck the ocean hissing. In the yard was the
Maypole Karna and I had put up the day before. I stood
at the window and looked out into the storm coming
toward us from the ocean and waited for her to come.
She was at a dance at the Lindberg Lodge where Swedes
and Norwegians and Finns used to go. They danced the
hambo and schottis and waltz and polka so Americans
were totally confused and I could almost hear them
laugh as I waited.

  I had been there when she celebrated Midsummer
Night. And there was no porridge. There was lobster

with mayonnaise, there was duck basted with cognac, and asparagus, and for dessert we ate strawberries in arrack and afterward I helped her wash the dishes. Then at eight in the evening she had taken the car and driven into Huntington and then to Lindberg Lodge for the dance. I had sat alone in the big room downstairs without turning on any lights and listened to "The Tiger Rag" while the midsummer darkness gathered around me. I sat too close to the record player and ran it on top speed. "The Tiger Rag" and "the Kazoo Moan" were probably the best pieces I knew. Karna could dance to those records too. If you played them at normal speed. Out there above the bay the storm came in from the ocean. And now at two in the morning Karna came home just as the thunderstorm began above us. I saw her come toward me across the yard in her white dancing dress. Her skirt swang and swept. I saw from the way she walked that she had danced the whole night and that was no surprise because whatever dance it was, foxtrot or waltz or another one, wherever they danced, at International House or Lindberg Lodge or some other place, Karna had to dance every dance. She was pretty when she laughed but didn't really know it herself. But I never told her or anyone else that I had stayed up waiting for her to come walking like that across the yard with her white dance dress swinging and sweeping around her legs and the red shoes dancing over the grass.

But here at Marieborg all the chairs scraped against the floor and the picture of Karna stuck to the window.

It stood still and in the middle of it a brown spot grew and grew and the film of Long Island ended where the time was still 1939 and it was night but here it was morning 1940 and there was a light yellow checked tablecloth on the dining room table and it appeared in the middle of the growing brown spot and took over and now the window was filled by the table with kids around it and the yard outside. Aunt Greta stood in the doorway and watched us and although we cousins were alone at the round table in the middle of the big dining room with all the empty tables around us we stood up now and shouted so everyone in the kitchen could hear:

"*Tack för maten, den var god!* Thanks for the meal. It tasted good!"

But we didn't have to fold our hands and thank God like in the Christian folk high schools.

It was Sunday morning and there was no course so the school was almost empty and I got away as soon as we had said our thanks for the meal—which in fact did not taste good and was nothing to be grateful for even if I should have remembered all the starving children out in Europe. I got up leaving the uneaten porridge and after saying thanks I acted as if I had happened to think of something, I snapped my fingers and nodded and then I had left my cousins and everything at the table and stood at the bulletin board right beside the door and looked like I was reading something there. When no one was looking in my direction I took two quiet barefoot steps backward—silently as a furtive Indian before the great defeat of the Sioux, I thought—and then slid around the corner into the corridor. No one called after me and I walked slowly up the steps to the school library in the attic. It was very quiet. I didn't hear anyone. Completely in peace. And it was so nice that I almost laughed, there was a tingling down my back all the way to my toes.

The room was lonely and bright. A slanted roof and windowseats. I felt the rag rugs under my toes. Newspapers lay in neat piles. Books were lined up in newly varnished wooden bookshelves, sun on the table and no one to bother me, just half-circle windows open to a blue sky and silent book spines facing me. I could stroke the spines of the books with my fingers and I could take my time. Take out a book. Think about what might be inside. Weigh it in my hand. Put it back again. Move on. Finally take a book to actually read. Sit down at the table. Open the book. Look around in the silence and feel the sunshine on my neck and then begin to read. And now the little blue book is open in front of me on the table.

But Aunt Greta was sharp, she knew where to look for me and she found me in the library and told me to rake the driveway because in the afternoon some women were coming. The students were away on break and it was going to be a housewives' meeting or a women's club meeting. It was not connected to the church and had nothing to do with spiritual preparedness and it was certainly not friendly toward Germany. But I had not listened carefully enough because I rescued myself at the last minute and she didn't see. I

had been reading a book when she came walking quietly up the stairs and forgot to be watchful enough so I
didn't hear her approach. I had barely been able to pull
a newspaper out of the pile to hide the book under the
Friday edition from Stockholm. At the same moment I
heard the tiles squeak outside I knew her hand was
already on the handle and that the door was about to fly
out and open the room around me.

I would act as if I was just reading the newspaper
and breathed like nothing was happening. Although
Greta stood there the words rose up from the page
toward me. I stared at the black text in the open newspaper in front of me and when I saw the words I
thought how happy the Hitler Hun was and how he let
joybells ring from all the churches as his soldiers goose-
stepped across Europe and how he held this Sweden in
his hand and how the Swedish blackcoats were not saying clearly how Hitler was a criminal and murderer who
ought to be punished and they didn't even dare talk
about his Germany as an *aggressor state* but prayed and
rang bells and walked away:

". . . godlessness and the selfishness which grows
out of it, individual as well as collective, is the real root
of all misery, including even war, and the true strength
of a people is the composure and assurance and the
unconquerable courage, which comes from the fellowship of faith in the living God . . ."

But I didn't show on my face what I was thinking
and I tried to look as though I was just reading idly. I
looked up at her when she came through the door and

raised my eyebrows so I would look a little bewildered. She didn't notice anything and when she told me to rake the yard she went away again and I could exhale. But I didn't breathe loudly enough for her to hear me and come back. Not that it really would have mattered if she had seen me reading and seen which book I was reading. It wasn't a strange book I was reading, nothing forbidden. It was a small blue book from the shelf for English language books. It was so small that I could almost put it in my pants pocket. If I had wanted to carry it away from there.

But I never wanted anyone to know what I was reading. When someone reached out a hand to take the book I was reading I froze up inside, gritted my teeth. It was like being stripped naked. They opened me up and looked inside me by seeing what I read. The little blue book was a book of ghost stories and things like that. It wasn't anything remarkable. Some pieces were boring or silly. It was really sad to read Le Fanu and writers like him. There were a few good pieces in the book. "The Facts in the Case of M. Waldemar" I had read several times before, I liked Edgar Allan Poe and knew his "The Raven" by heart. Anyway, I almost did. I liked H.G. Wells too. *The Time Machine* and things like that by him were good. But his world history was wordy. Now I had just finished reading his story about the door in the wall when I realized Aunt Greta was opening the door. The words still echoed around me.

"By our daylight standards he walked out of security into darkness, danger and death. But did he see

it like that?"

That stuck on my lips and the hairs on my neck stood straight out and the words rushed through my whole body and the door in the wall stood open there in front of me leading to a kind of park in all its dazzling magnificence and just at that moment I heard the floor tiles squeak and knew that Aunt Greta was coming now. So I pulled the newspaper toward me and acted like nothing was happening. Never would she discover me, have the chance to look straight into me. And I imagined what she would say. She could certainly talk about H.G. Wells. And I knew how she would ask what a twelve-year-old could possibly like about him and I heard her auntlike drilling cold curiosity voice and my teeth tingled and that was why I hid the book I was reading with the Friday paper from Stockholm and smiled at her and raised my eyebrows a little to look bewildered and breathed as if it were nothing.

Yes, I heard her say I should rake the yard. After she left I didn't remember so clearly the other things she said. The Women's Services ladies were probably not coming today because they had been here the week before. It wasn't a church group either. Robert and Greta weren't like that anyway. But it was women. They would have some kind of coffee down in the manor house garden facing Bråviken and they would bring some sweet rolls.

I put down the newspaper. But I didn't steal the book. Not this time anyway. I was going down to rake. But I put it up high on top of the yellow cabinet. Where

I could see it. There were going to be other visitors to the library one of these days. Maybe I should let it get lost. But it must not be found in my luggage or in my room. After a month or so I could move it somewhere else if I wanted to. And in the fall I could take it with me. If I wanted to. Then I closed the library and went down the steps.

I was walking across the gravel now under the huge lindens and pulled the big rake behind me. It was heavy and its heavy wooden tines wrote deep lines in the gravel. I made them draw a grid in front of the white facade with the tall glass windows. And up from the gables up there the round attic windows looked down on the pyre. And now all the lindens bent over me and I pulled and pulled. When I turned the rake I lifted it up and carried it in my arms onto the grass so I could set it down exactly with the inside tine in the outside furrow so the big grill where France would be cooked would not look plowed out like a field with turn-around snakes.

Now all the churchbells rang out above the virgin and with heavy steps she walked to the pyre. Joan, you good woman, you save France with your death. Now I walk alone here under the lindens and because no one can hear me I practice shouting at the audience in a loud voice.

"What do they all amount to, these kings and captains and bishops and lawyers and such like? They just leave you in the ditch to bleed to death."

I drag the rake behind me in silence but all this doesn't really exist and I'm standing in the black midsummer night at the window in my room on Long Island last year when there was no war yet and look at the fireflies out there and wait for Karna to come home or maybe I'm dreaming or I'm lying on the beach rolling a red stone and imagining all this with Sweden and Marieborg and Aunt Greta and all that. But that's not how it was. I knew that. That's not how it was. All this here was reality. *There is no hiding place.*

There was sighing in the treetops.

"The wind warns of the coming storm," I said aloud although no one could hear me.

There were more clouds now. They gathered into a dark tower. The rake dug deep furrows in the gravel behind me. There are some good examples. As Mr. Flourens told me now as he walked beside me with his hands at his back.

"It is doubtful that James Watt ever understood algebra. In any case he didn't make use of it. Have you thought, my young friend, that if James Watt had been able to study and participate in the banal intellectual life of Oxford he would have become a learned professor who wrote his equations in proper form. But because he had the advantage of working outside the established rules he was able to take a superior view and shaped a whole century. It is therefore no coincidence that he preferred Shakespeare to Racine!

"Genius," he said as he trotted beside me while I bent forward, pulling my heavy rake. *"A genius like James Watt proves itself by* overstepping *common sense* and general opinion and it refuses to be locked up in the little intellectual pens of schools and universities."

Here as I walked beside Mr. Flourens in Sweden I could suddenly say it out loud to myself although before I hadn't wanted to let on about it:

"This baldheaded, chubby engineer without real academic credentials whom I called Mr. Flourens, he doesn't really exist and has never existed for the others out in reality. He just walks here beside me speaking from books!"

Mr. Flourens became almost angry when I said that. He shook his hand in the air and stamped his feet so the gravel scattered around his heels.

"The fledgeling lispeth his opinions, said he. For shame! Why dost thou not keep a more civil tongue in thy head? Hast thou not read what the Author of Waverly *wrote to Captain Cuthbert Clutterbuck about his meeting with James Watt for whom nothing human was alien?"*

"Yes," I said and turned toward Mr. Flourens who trudged forward at my side. "Of course I've read Walter Scott's *The Monastery* even though I don't like books where white ladies haunt the plot. And the songs she sings are tiresome. But Halbert Glendinning I like and he dove into the water so smartly the night he left the Castle of Avenel."

"Here thou spakest empty words like the young fool that thou art," said Mr. Flourens.

Now I heard a strong wind in the treetops above me and the gravel crunched and I felt great sorrow because I knew what he would say:

"You are like Captain Clutterbuck, I said, you Mr.

Flourens belong to the Kingdom of Nowhere."

And when I had said that he went completely away all at once although I've had him almost a year. He had told me a lot although he was just an imaginary man. I walked there all alone and dragged the rake behind me and knew that he would never come back. But Mr. Flourens didn't fit in Sweden. I tried to tell myself he didn't like being in Europe now that there was war. But it didn't work any more to think that. To be able to pretend you have to avoid speaking out loud so you can hear yourself pretending. If you hear it, the door to pretending closes altogether. In a way I was talking about fairy tales, I thought. That's why the troll dies when you say the troll's name. When you pretend, you must never pretend that you are pretending. Then the pretending bursts.

But Mr. Flourens had in fact not fit at all in Sweden. Actually I had already stopped making him appear on the ship. And that was why he became angry and started to talk so strangely with "thou" and "thine" and words like that when I let him come out. But he had often been fun during the year I had him. And smart too. And taught me a lot. But it was getting to be difficult to even remember him any more I noticed. I didn't see him any more. Didn't remember how he had looked other than pale and colorless. It was as if the whole thought called Mr. Flourens had ended. As if it started to close up when I got on the ship and as if I had turned off a faucet forever when I told him directly that he was just imaginary. I walked there all alone with the rake under the lindens and you could hear in the lindens above me that there would probably be thunder this afternoon.

When I turned and looked around the whole big driveway was properly raked and from the big house someone called me to come and eat. There was spinach in white sauce with blood pudding and lingonberries first and processed sour milk afterward.

The women came to the garden party after we had eaten the blood pudding and sour milk and Aunt Greta forbade me to dip bread in the milk.

"Don't make a mess!"

The women walked around in the yard. I sat with Grandmother on the terrace and drank raspberry juice and looked at them. Grandmother read yesterday's newspaper. Chicken-run! The women walked around down on the lawn and cackled. And suddenly all this cackling motion stopped. I made them stand still. Froze the picture like a film that has stuck. Everything is still and bright on the table a few moments before a black rose opens up in the middle of the picture, one that starts to burn with brown leaves. I couldn't make time stand still, but it burned. I widened the moment, opened it and stepped through it down the steps and across the lawn out to the women.

They stood completely motionless with open eyes. The one with the long dark hair, the wide blue skirt and the short-sleeved white blouse held the coffee cup with her left hand outstretched and her skirt rose up in the wind like on the girl in John Sloan who walked down the subway steps at 42nd Street and which I had tacked on the inside of my closet door at home in New York. If Karna had still been in America she would have been able to see it. But now since the Irishwoman had come to our house I had started to lock even the closet. Every time I opened the closet door the skirt was raised up in the wind and the girl looked at me. It had been in a book Gunnar got for Christmas 1939 from his secretary called *A Treasury of American Prints* and it had many good pictures. It wasn't a real book but more like an unbound collection of a hundred signed prints by various living American graphic artists. I could take them out without him or Alva noticing anything. They never looked at books like that after they got them.

Actually it was another picture I had wanted to put up. It was by Reginald Marsh and was called "Star Burlesque" and was of a burlesque dancer, one of those with just a little g-string down there and who was doing *a bump and a real grind* for an audience of whooping and screaming men while the music just rolled on. But I didn't dare put it up. No lock was really safe. If they caught me they would say something. Maybe even Karna would have said something if I'd had a picture like that tacked up where she could see I had tacked it up. Teased me or something. Matisse on the wall would have to do, with Sloan in the closet. I could at least look at the other pictures, Marsh and ones like that. I had taken possession of them and stuffed them in together with several issues of *Peep Show* which were not art at all and all the other scraps of paper among the bundles of *Model Railroader, Model Builder, Life* and *Fortune* and others beside my piles of books on the white shelves next to my bed. They would never search there because it was visible and not hidden away. And what anyone could see was the safest hiding place as Poe demonstrated in "The Purloined Letter" I thought.

Now I had made time stand still around all of them there on the lawn. When I came closer to the one with the dark hair and reached out my hand toward her to touch it I noticed how the moment began to pull itself together, time throbbed and I was forced up onto the terrace again to avoid getting caught in there.

"It's horrible in the world," said Grandmother and looked up from the newspaper. "It's become so you can't believe how horrible things are when it's so peaceful here."

Or think of it another way. I took out the little brown drop bottle with *the new accelerator* and let the green drops fall slowly down into the juice glass one after the other. I counted eleven drops and put the dropper back into the brown bottle. I thought for a brief moment. Then I swallowed the bitter drink all in one gulp. You have to close your eyes when the decoction begins to work. It rushes to the head and everything heaves around you. It feels like being on a boat in a storm. Like on the *Mathilda Thordén* when we passed Iceland in the spring storms. But when everything was quiet I could open my eyes again and I lived many thousands of times faster than all the others. Grandmother was sitting right beside me. She had put down the newspaper and looked at me and had opened her mouth to tell me something. But not a sound was heard. I held the juice glass in my right hand and a drop hung in the air directly below the glass. I realized it was falling toward the table. But I didn't see it move. I lost my grip on the empty juice glass but it didn't fall, it rested motionless in the air. Down below all life had stopped. The women stood there like statues. I got up and went down the steps and out onto the lawn. I moved so quickly now that the grass was singed and turned brown under the soles of my feet.

The women stood completely still. They were like plaster castings of the people who were surprised by sudden death one day in Pompeii like the pictures in the history books at school. Only the plaster had been painted. Some were blonde, others brunette and a few red-haired. Some grinned with faces petrified in grimaces, others were talking and their mouths had stayed wide open in the middle of a sentence. I could see down into their throats. Count the fillings in their teeth. But all sound had quieted. Only the hollow ratatata of a cricket. Most of the women were ugly. I looked at them one after the other. I went up close to them. Examined their faces. Big blackheads, blemishes on their faces although they tried to powder over them and pimples on the backs of their necks under their hair. Twenty-five statues with arms spread. The pretty one with the wide blue skirt and the short-sleeved white blouse had managed to put down her coffee cup while I was up on the terrace that short while and she had been in the middle of turning around and held her skirt down with her hand, the thick dark hair had blown across her face so you couldn't see her eyes or mouth. The big-eyed and younger teen-aged girl with blonde bangs beside her looked unseeing straight ahead over her shoulder at me. It was like in "Mala Noche" only it was dark hair and not the white veil that was caught by the wind and hid the woman's face.

Now she wasn't at all the girl in Sloan's picture, now I recognized her from Goya's picture. He did a different kind of picture. Sloan's pictures moved when you looked at them a while but Goya's pictures opened inward. At home in New York I used to lie on the floor in my room and look at his pictures. You could fantasize in a special way with them. Hear the figures talk. And they hadn't even noticed when that book too was gone from their bookshelves when they packed and that I had put this big Goya book in my luggage with the whole collection of American prints and the Bruegel picture book and Holbein and all the others. All this without them knowing. They didn't really like books and thought that among my books were only things like Booth Tarkington's Penrod books. When they paid so little attention to pictures like that it was right that I should take the books they had been given.

I stood and looked a while at the dark woman. I altered the picture. Now while I stood like this close to her and could look right at her without anyone noticing—as if she were a picture—I could see the body under the clothes. I reached my hand out toward the dark windblown hair to touch it, to lift it and see her

face, but she existed in their time which went many
thousands of times more slowly than my time, the hair
was a carpet of stone. Her face was hidden by a dark
stone wall. When I put my hand on her skirt it was blue
skirt fabric like tank armor and when I touched her skin
it was very hard and ice cold as stainless steel. Her lips
were like red marble against my fingertips when I
touched them.

I walked around the yard and looked at the women.
And one evening as I sat in Karna's room and talked
with Karna about what we did with the girls up in our
secret fort under the Riverside Drive viaduct at 125th
Street she laughed and said:

"You know, Jan, you remind me of when Kålle
went shopping at the department store."

"Oh, Karna!" said Ingrid, who had just come into
the room.

"Yes, one day Kålle went to the department store
and asked for something in a box way up under the ceiling and Ada who was serving him climbed up the ladder
to get it down and Kålle leaned forward and looked up
at her as she climbed the ladder.

"Karna!" said Ingrid.

"He won't die from hearing it," said Karna. "You
don't know Jan like I do. Anyway, Kålle looked up at
Ada as she climbed and when she came down and he
had paid Kålle put an extra five on the counter and said
it was so Ada could buy some underpants. Ada told the
other salesgirls about this and the next time Kålle came in
they all climbed up on ladders. Kålle went and looked up

at them one after the other and looked thoughtful and
when he had paid and was ready to go he put one crown
on the counter and said: 'I can't afford underpants for all
of you but you can at least buy a five-öre hairnet."

"That was twenty hairnets," I said. "Ada and nineteen
other girls climbed up on twenty ladders and Kålle
walked underneath and looked at them all."

Ingrid had blushed and left the room but Karna had
just laughed and ruffled my hair. All that evening and the
whole night and the next day I felt her hand as she ruffled
my hair and I had thought of Stella but no longer.
Suddenly now as I looked at the women I knew it was
wrong to think of her. She didn't exist any more either.
But I don't want to say that.

I couldn't look at the women in the yard the way
Kålle had done. They existed in another time speed and
stood wrapped in their tank armor dresses. I couldn't see
them move. I did notice that a hand moved suddenly now
and as I walked back to the girl with the blue skirt I saw
that the dark stone wall hair that blew in their time now
looked different than before. I could see her eyes. The
women were moving! But they moved as slowly as glaci-
ers move and even if I walked right up to the women
who stood with bare faces and open eyes and looked
right into their open eyes there was no sight in them and
now Grandmother put her hand on my shoulder and said:

"You look so dreamy, Jan. What are you thinking
about?"

"Nothing," I said.

Because it was both Stella and hairnets for all of

them I was thinking about and I tried now to see Karna instead although I knew I shouldn't do that and suddenly I felt her hand through my hair but all at once the hand was gone and I noticed how I jumped and almost lost my breath and it wasn't possible to see anything anymore. She didn't come walking across the driveway. But it was only words. It was with her like it was with Mr. Flourens. There was only a colorless and blurred picture of words.

Yes, Karna was gone although she had really existed last year and was probably still somewhere in this Sweden. Thirty weeks and one day had passed since Karna had departed forever. She hadn't gone to Sweden because of the war. It was Ingrid who had wanted to go home. She was engaged in Sweden too. Karna had decided to stay in America. She wanted to finish her degree at the university. Then we shall see, she said. But she got a little sick and was forced to live on milk and toast and sausage and it was no fun. She got tired of it. And so Ingrid had persuaded her. She talked to Karna as though it were for our sake and not for her own that she planned to stay in America despite the war in Europe. You have to think more about yourself than about the Myrdals, said Ingrid. And so Karna decided to go with Ingrid back to Sweden.

That was how she left. I went with her in the car down to the dock and then I was among all the others who said goodbye to her and Ingrid up on the tourist deck aboard the SS *Stavanger*. It was full of people from International House and many of Karna's friends and

Gunnar's secretary Miss Dornbrush. Alva was also there to say goodbye and wish them a happy trip. The departure whistle blew and all visitors had to leave the ship. I stayed on the dock in New York and watched Karna wave with her handkerchief as the SS *Stavanger* shoved off. I neither cried nor laughed then. I knew she was leaving forever but when I tried to feel something, nothing was there. I was neither sad nor happy. I was nothing and I watched the handkerchief wave for a long time until it was just a ship far away and I turned in toward the city again. That evening I stayed in my room and listened to "The Lone Ranger" and then read some of *Penrod Jashber* which was the kind of book you could read many times, now and then, here and there and I thought it was strange not to feel more when people disappear for the rest of your life. As if they died. And now she was all gone. Forever and it was I who did it. I should not have tried to visualize her again. Not any more. It went wrong. Karna had been emptied out, she had become just empty words like Mr. Flourens.

"Nothing," I said. "I'm not thinking about anything special."

It came from far away and throbbed over me again . Like big dark wings. Like big claws opened toward me. Came from far away and washed over me at Bråviken. Around me was like a steel cage. And there were no real colors any more. Everything was completely lifeless and still as usual. Down there the women-hens cackled. Grandmother poured more juice. She meant well. But she didn't understand anything.

"The children are so sweet," she said to Aunt Elsa.
"And Jan, of course, is the easiest one to take care of."

I waited for the thunder rumbling far away. The
land around the terrace lay in the gray light of heat with
gray haze down by Bråviken. I didn't even see the cage
anymore. That too was just words. But I felt the big dark
wings flap. The crowd of women cackled. Now as I listened to the cackling they looked different too. Even the
one in the blue skirt had a shrill voice. I tried one more
time to change the picture in front of me but it was stuck
and now rigid and unmoving. I couldn't change anything
in it and no matter how I strained my eyes the cackling
women continued to mince around. Marieborg was a
gray stifling veil around me. Time had closed in around
me. And I would never get out of it. I was stuck in
Sweden. Stuck forever.

"I'll never get out of this. There's no way back."

And now I sat there and wept, but I wept with dry
open eyes because no one must notice that I was weeping and no one would, never would anyone know.

♦ ♦ ♦